simple hospitality

JANE JARRELL

W PUBLISHING GROUP
A Division of Thomas Nelson Publishers
Since 1798

www.wpublishinggroup.com

SIMPLE HOSPITALITY

Published by W Publishing Group, a Division of Thomas Nelson, Inc., P.O. Box 141000, Nashville, Tennessee 37214.

W Publishing Group books may be purchased in bulk for educational, business, fund-raising, or sales promotional use. For information, please e-mail SpecialMarkets@ThomasNelson.com.

All Scripture quotations, unless otherwise indicated, are taken from The Holy Bible, New International Version. Copyright ©1973, 1978, 1984, International Bible Society. Used by permission of Zondervan Bible Publishers.

Other Scripture quotations are taken from the following sources: The New Century Version® (NCV). Copyright © 1987, 1988, 1991 by Word Publishing, a Division of Thomas Nelson, Inc. Used by permission. All rights reserved. The New King James Version (NKJV®), copyright 1979, 1980, 1982, Thomas Nelson, Inc., Publishers. The New American Standard Bible (NASB), ©1960, 1977 by the Lockman Foundation.

Library of Congress Cataloging-in-Publication Data

Jarrell, Jane Cabaniss, 1961–
  Simple hospitality / by Jane Jarrell.
    p. cm.
  ISBN 0-8499-0484-6
  1. Home economics. 2. Hospitality—Religious aspects—Christianity. 3. Women—Religious life. I. Title.
TX147.J37 2005
640—dc22
2004029465

Printed in the United States of America
05 06 07 08 09 VG 9 8 7 6 5 4 3 2 1

For my loving in-laws,
Keith and Allegra Jarrell.
Your love, kindness, generosity, and compassion have consistently shown
the true meaning of hospitality in my life.
Thank you.

Contents

꿎

Acknowledgments

Thank You, God, for allowing this project to make it through the finish line.

Thank you to the professional, helpful, and caring staff at W Publishing Group. Debbie Wickwire, you did it again; thank you for the prayer and energy you put into your projects and to those people involved. Laura Kendall, your enthusiasm and skilled book coordination make working with you a pleasure. Jennifer Stair, you are a detail diva, dotting i's and crossing t's to make a manuscript smooth as rich chocolate. I feel much gratitude toward you leading ladies.

Sabra Smith Inzer, your art has always been my favorite. Your friendship has always been treasured. Thank you for adding style to the pages with your talented hands.

Finally, thank you to my parents, Bill and Sarah Cabaniss, who have always created an atmosphere of hospitality in their home.

Pure Hospitality

What's the first thing that comes to your mind when you think of the word *hospitality*? Is it June Cleaver standing at the front door with a large platter of freshly baked cookies? A spotless home free of clutter? A chicken spaghetti casserole on its way out the door for a sick friend? Entertaining a group in your home with fancy foods and creative tabletops?

Hospitality can be all of the above, yet it could also be none of the above. So what is hospitality, and how does one simplify the process? We're going to be defining—and redefining—hospitality throughout this book. But let's start with a definition from Webster: "To be hospitable is to be disposed to behave in a warm way and manner, and to entertain with generous sensitivity, availability and kindness."[1] Warm. Generous. Sensitive. Available. Kind. These words are what hospitality is all about. At its core, hospitality is about sharing God's love with others.

But today, many of us don't think we have the time for hospitality. We may not think we have the skills, the expertise, or the ideas. We might not be aware of the tremendous rewards found in sharing hospitality with others. We often think it takes too much effort. We think, *I just don't have the gift of hospitality.*

Simple Hospitality is here to offer encouragement. I can't take away all your responsibilities, manage your time, or know who might need your act of kindness today. But I can share ideas and experiences to help you find a hospitality style that works for you, no matter how hectic your life, no matter how "hospitality challenged" you think you are. My intent in this book is to help you maximize your minutes as well as your ministry—your hospitality ministry.

Hospitality is as simple as a smile. It is as easy as popping the lid of a cold soft drink for another. It is as refreshing as a heart-to-heart conversation with a friend. The heart of hospitality is the art of developing caring relationships. Hospitality says, "We love you, you are welcome, and we want you to enjoy our home, food, and fellowship." It is reaching out to a friend or a family member who needs to feel accepted, loved, and cared for. It is opening your arms to the less fortunate and loving people through difficult circumstances. It is caring for young children when a mother is at her wit's end. It is a pot of beef stew or a bucket of chicken when a neighbor moves in next-door. When we offer our homes and our lives to others, we are acting according to Scripture, which tells us, "Love must be sincere. . . . Be devoted to one another in brotherly love. Honor one another above yourselves. . . . Share with God's people who are in need. Practice hospitality" (Romans 12:9–10, 13). Real Christian hospitality isn't an option; it is what God commands.

But many of us still think hospitality is anything but simple. We each have our own backgrounds and preconceived notions of hospitality. I was no exception. It has only been in the last few years that I've discovered that hospitality can truly be *simple*.

FAMILY MATTERS

I grew up entertaining. My parents were in the ministry until I was ten, so we often had groups over for snacks, meals, and fellowship. My most beloved memories with friends and family usually occurred during impromptu get-togethers. A stack of paper plates, plastic forks, chilled sodas, and sandwich fixings made for a great time.

After working with a food magazine, I began to feel a certain pressure to show off when entertaining. I thought people expected "the works" from me: a spotless and beautiful home, unique place settings, cutting-edge foods, and elegant desserts. The pressure to have everything just right really stressed me out and dissolved the pleasure of pure hospitality. Honestly, to this day I feel a perfectionist twinge to make it all just right.

Many times, I'm not relaxed because I have a picture in my mind of "the perfect hostess." I think my friends and family must perceive me as an incredibly gifted, talented, creative entertainer and chef in order to be impressed and happy. Fellow hostesses, it is time to take that perfect picture off the wall of our minds and put up a plaque that reads: *The key to any act of hospitality is the kind and loving spirit I give as a gift to my friends, family members, and even those I don't know.*

As we remove the entertaining aspect from hospitality, we move toward offering ourselves as real people sharing God's love. When we take the focus off ourselves, we find an incredible joy in comforting others.

Hospitality does not try to impress but to serve. Entertaining puts things before people, but hospitality does the opposite. Hospitality does everything with no thought of external reward. Instead it takes pleasure in the joy of giving, doing, loving, and serving. Because hospitality has put away its pride, it doesn't care if others see our humanness. We are maintaining no false pretension; people relax and enjoy our offer of friendship. When we are being truly hospitable, we forgo the urge to "wow."

HISTORICAL HOSPITALITY

Many of us grew up hearing the biblical stories of hospitality. Abraham welcomed three strangers who turned out to be angels dropping by to tell Abraham and Sarah that they would have a son. Mary and Martha opened their home to Jesus and His followers—a large group for whom to prepare an impromptu meal! Remember the two men on the road to Emmaus? They asked a stranger to join them for dinner. Afterward they realized that this stranger was the risen Jesus!

When we welcome guests, we are blessed in surprising ways. When we share love or do something for others, we reap the benefits of more love in our lives and we store up treasure in heaven. We can become true servants in both word and deed. Whether we serve our friends, our children, our neighbors, our family members, or strangers, we should keep in mind the words Jesus spoke: "I tell you the truth, whatever you did for one of the least of these brothers of mine, you did for me" (Matthew 25:40).

EFFECTIVE USE OF THIS BOOK

I have designed this book with your lifestyle in mind. Please don't feel like you have to read all fourteen chapters in order! Each chapter is broken down into short, manageable sections packed full of ideas, so you can read a little bit here and there when you have time. You'll find heart care scriptures, home care ideas, quick cleaning fixes, simple recipes, decorating ideas, kid connections, and more. Select a few ideas that work for you, or use them as springboards for your own creative thoughts. We'll start in chapter 1 with ideas for addressing our own hearts so we are better equipped to focus on our families and then others.

I pray that this book will help you in your journey toward intentionally sharing yourself and your home with others. Thanks for taking me along with you! Let's get started.

PART ONE

Keep It Simple

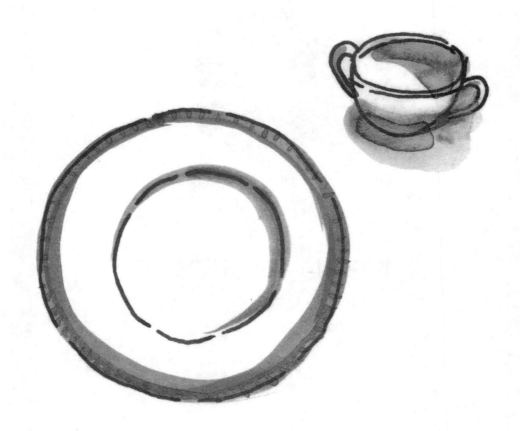

CHAPTER ONE

Clean Plate Club

God has a history of using the insignificant to accomplish the impossible.
—RICHARD EXLEY

Women play multiple roles in life, from caregiver to coach, often with no time to assess our personal heart desires. Can we simply have too much on our plates? Some people's lives remind me of the paper plate commercial in which a flimsy paper plate is piled full of entrées. In an attempt to satisfy, more and more is piled on the plate. But before reaching the table, the plate collapses under the pressure of oversized servings. The same is true for our lives: with a flimsy foundation, we fold under the pressures, obligations, and commitments. Chinet to the rescue! This strong paper plate provides a solid foundation for the food and doesn't collapse when overloaded. Likewise, God provides a strong foundation for our lives. He encourages us to lighten our load, and He supports us as we try to focus on eternal heart issues while providing strength for our overbooked lives.

To accomplish all we find on our plates, we must tap into the resources available only through supernatural power. Are you still using a flimsy plate, pulling on your limited personal resources, or have you found the strong plate by relying on God's strength to meet the challenges?

In this chapter we are going to examine our deepest inner life. I've always liked interior design! We'll do a little spring-cleaning and maybe some polishing as we seek to become God's best.

What does this have to do with hospitality? Plenty. We can't give love, share empathy, or offer intimacy to another if we are carrying the weight of the world on our plates. If we're overloaded, we're not equipped to offer heartfelt hospitality to those we care about. If we're too wound up in our own issues, hurdles, and obligations, we have no space to focus on the needs of the world around us. To avoid this dilemma we must work from the inside out. Are you ready to belong to the clean plate club?

HEART CHECK

As wives and mothers, we're often told, "You have to take care of yourself first!" But we all know that usually doesn't happen. We spend most of our time staying on top of the needs of our families. Yet there is truth in that advice! To provide a loving environment at home and to be a role model for loving others through hospitality, we must start with our own hearts. We can't afford to let ourselves get out of shape, spiritually speaking.

Every now and then I find myself with some "heart" problems no beta blocker can touch. I may be so stressed out that I can't find time for prayer or personal worship and study. My overwhelming responsibilities might create resentment. Difficult circumstances in my family can lead to loss of hope. We all know that life annoyances like these can stack up like bricks and weigh heavily on our lives. Getting through these situations often takes an all-out attack—a heart attack!

How does one launch an all-out heart attack? Here's my four-step, straight-A plan for dealing with those issues of the heart that can rob the joy from our lives, squelch our effectiveness, and keep us from sharing love with others.

HOW TO LAUNCH AN ALL-OUT HEART ATTACK

ASSESS

ADDRESS

ANTICIPATE

ABIDE

ASSESS

First, evaluate your current heart condition. Are your arteries clogged up? In other words, is there too much "stuff" in your life, keeping you from functioning most effectively? If so, it may be time for a priority check.

You will need a notepad, some scheduled time alone, and your Bible. Begin by asking yourself, what's most important to me? Then ask, how do I spend my time? Making the effort to reflect on how your actions match up with your stated priorities is often enlightening. However, I don't want this to become a guilt trip for you! This exercise is just a way of discovering the areas of your life that could be tweaked a bit to bring you closer to living your priorities. Make a list of the areas that seem to be working well and areas that feel out of control. The goal is to assess yourself, beginning with the good and ending with the opportunity for change.

In John 15:1–2, Jesus says, "I am the true vine; my Father is the gardener. He cuts off every branch of mine that does not produce fruit" (NCV). This is God's assessing. What works, stays. What doesn't work is cut off. Is there anything in your life that needs to be "cut off" so you are able to produce more?

This self-assessment can become a habit—a system of checks and balances for your life. Using this thought process allows you to stay focused on what works and to identify when something isn't working so you can change course.

ADDRESS

Once you have assessed, you have clarity for conquering your situation. Clarity gives us the ability to deal with what's in front of us. Without it, our vision is limited. In John 15:2, Jesus says, "He trims and cleans every branch that produces fruit so that it will produce even more fruit." Addressing your issues allows for a clean heart and the opportunity for more fruit production. What fruit can God produce through a cleaned-up you?

Julia, a mother of three, found herself constantly bombarded with family problems that were a daily drain on her emotional energy. After living this way for years, she came to the realization that she needed to take action. She took out a yellow legal pad and began writing all the negative situations she had to endure. She also wrote down the positive things in her life—activities that, while worthy, also took up time. Then she realistically looked at her options, asking the question, what can be removed? She set about preparing a plan to live more according to her priorities. It took time. It also took some negotiating with family members and others to whom she'd made commitments. But in time, she found her life running more smoothly, and she found a new sense of peace. Did her problems go away? No. But assessing and addressing the issues gave her the opportunity to see, for the first time, exactly what changes were needed.

When I feel my life is spinning out of control, I sit down with my personal "housecleaning" verses: "God, examine me and know my heart; test me and know my nervous thoughts. See if there is any bad thing in me. Lead me on the road to everlasting life" (Psalm 139:23–24 NCV). To become all God has created me to be, I need to approach my life with a clean conscience (or plate). I start by confessing the known sins in my life and by forgiving others I feel have wronged me. I find that staying spiritually "clean" is similar to housework: if I don't stay on top of the "mess" daily, I find myself buried under the bundle of burdens! Once I "address the mess" through confession, I'm ready to begin working with God to trim the branches of my life so that I'm refreshed and my fruit will be pleasing to Him. When we are spiritually fresh, we have the God-given ability to refresh others; thus, the first seeds are planted for sowing hospitality into our hearts and into the hearts of others.

ANTICIPATE

When you're starting to make changes in your life, you can anticipate challenges. Whether God is testing you on your resolve or Satan is throwing down roadblocks to keep you from being your most effective self, if you anticipate certain issues you will not be as disappointed in the midst of change. This keeps you on your toes and ready to push toward your resolve.

What are some challenges you might anticipate? You might expect the protests of family members who are used to you doing things a certain way. If you decide to step down from a leadership or volunteer position, you may face the disappointment or disapproval of people you respect. Most of all, you may find yourself confronted with your own guilt or sense of failure for not being superwoman. I urge you not to back down in the face of these roadblocks but to pray continually about your decisions and stick to them, as long as you have peace that they're the right choices. The obstacles will be easier to deal with if you have anticipated them.

How do we know *what* to anticipate? Review your history and the patterns you follow when dealing with change. Consider who will be affected by the changes you'll be making, and what their responses are likely to be. Keep in mind that, often, the reality is not as bad as your imagination! Yet the road is generally easier if we've anticipated the roadblocks.

ABIDE

Through all the assessing, addressing, and anticipating, we abide. Abiding in Christ is like being in a quiet, candlelit room, tucked into a cozy, overstuffed bed in the middle of a raging storm. Christ is the down comforter wrapped all around you, shielding you from the elements. In John 15:4, Jesus tells us, "Remain in me, and I will remain in you. A branch cannot produce fruit alone but must remain in the vine. In the same way, you cannot produce fruit alone but must remain in me" (NCV).

We cannot accurately assess, address, or anticipate unless we remain in Christ. When He is on the throne of our hearts, we are more likely to make the right decisions, clearing our schedules and opening our hearts to be ready to reach out to others.

HEART RHYTHMS

As we go through the process of assessing and addressing, we must identify our priorities. Living our priorities is critical to controlling the stress level in our lives. When we get in touch with the things that are truly important, our priorities become the compass by which we chart our lives.

But how do we set our priorities? In his excellent book *Freedom from Tyranny of the Urgent*, Charles Hummel tells us, "There is no blueprint for all Christians in the use of their time, any more than there is for spending their money. God has given us widely differing abilities, amounts of energy, opportunities, responsibilities and personal needs. In that light, instead of comparing yourself to someone else, realistically consider the basic components of what for you is a productive Christian life. Ask God, 'What are Your priorities for me right now?' You can then prayerfully set appropriate personal goals."[1]

For our heart rhythms to stay in sync, we must focus. As a busy mother, I find focusing to be difficult. (My theory is that brain cells are reduced during the delivery of a baby!) Focus is one of the most challenging aspects of my daily life. I might carefully plan my day, but it spins into orbit at the onset of my child's ear infection or an unexpected need at the school. How do I stay on track? I find that to focus well means I must first know *what* to focus *on*—and that brings us back to priorities.

I need to regularly revisit my priorities. Not only do I need reminders, but my priorities also tend to change over time. To determine my priorities, I use the following simple yet thought-provoking exercise. It can be an eyeopener. Try this prayerfully and see how God speaks to you.

On a sheet of paper, make four columns, using each of the following questions as a column heading:

1. What do I want to do?
2. What do I want to be?
3. What do I want to have?
4. Whom do I want to help?

Write your answers beneath each heading. Dig deep and see what you find. Then narrow your answers to four words that sum up your columns. When you have four words, select one that represents you. While obviously your existence is not this simple, this exercise is a good way to mirror your heart. As I completed this exercise, my four words were *heart, compassion, home,* and *hospitality.* My one word was *share.* As I go through my days, when I feel like I'm getting too scattered, I go back to these words, and they help me focus on the important things in my life.

Adjusting priorities is a daily decision—a decision that should involve placing your focus on God instead of the circumstances at hand. Life happens, and when it does, our priorities can spin out of control. Plates that are too full or hearts that are too heavy can bring an onset of priority paralysis. When I begin to feel like the little ball batted around in a pinball machine, hitting off one corner and slamming into another one, I know God is not in control. As the bells and whistles begin to ring, I realize I am following my will and not God's. This is when critical assessment is in order—restructuring what is truly important and renewing my focus toward eternity.

When I suffer from priority paralysis, I stop, quickly review what is important, and rearrange the thought processes that are fogging the issue. A powerful prayer, a focus on obedience, and a heart choice can slow the spin and calm our spirits. These are quick and easy steps to clarify our thinking.

THREE STEPS TO CLARIFY OUR THINKING

A POWERFUL PRAYER
A FOCUS ON OBEDIENCE
A HEART CHOICE

Hospitality starts in our hearts. We are better able to see a need and reach a person when we know where we are coming from and whom we serve. This is a crucial starting point, doing some inside work so we are equipped to make a difference in the outside world.

The thing you should want most is God's kingdom and doing what God wants. Then all these other things you need will be given to you.

—Matthew 6:33 NCV

SIMPLE SOLUTIONS

1. Find your satisfaction in Christ instead of in the barrenness of being busy.
2. Create a checks-and-balances system for keeping your plate clean. Keep what is working, and remove those obligations that are driven by guilt or unhealthy assumptions.
3. When reviewing what piles are on your plate, talk with a trusted friend and consider her input as valuable insight. Our friends often see our circumstances more clearly than we can.
4. Choose to dwell on what is good in your life while you are working on your interior design.
5. Strive to look at life through an eternal lens with the goal of making all your choices glorifying to God.
6. Consistently ask God, "What are Your priorities for me today?"
7. Take time to offer yourself spiritual hospitality—abide and decide how God can use you today.

CHAPTER TWO

The Simple Truth

Kindness can conquer the most trying of situations.

Hospitality is kindness extended in myriad ways: A burning porch light. A table full of food. A hug. A get-together for children. A clean house. Coffee brewing in the kitchen. Gracious hospitality offers comfort, encouragement, and forgiveness in a generous fashion. It is allowing the spirit of God to flow through you by putting others before yourself.

You may not feel you're gifted or talented in the area of hospitality. It doesn't matter! We have no idea how God will use us if we just *show up*. It is as simple as that! We view things with a human perspective, but God sees our sphere of influence, our purpose for being on the planet, and what He can accomplish through us. He has the ability to take the ordinary and make it extraordinary. The smallest gesture of reaching out toward another person can have the most astonishing results. What design does God have on your life? How does He want to use you to reach others?

I believe God *does* want to use you—but He doesn't require you to change who you are. He can work through you to reach others in small ways, if simplicity is your style.

In this chapter, I have taken the word *hospitality* and made it into an acrostic to help us remember how simple it can be. When we take the focus off our circumstances and turn our hearts toward God and others, it's amazing how much easier hospitality looks. Look at this as a road map for sharing yourself with others.

H—HOSPITAL FOR THE SOUL

Why does one go to the hospital? To visit, perhaps, or to welcome a new baby. But oftentimes it's because our bodies are broken. Broken by disease, accident, or age. A hospital is a place to be repaired and healed.

The word *hospitable* is derived from the word *hospital*, which means a charitable institution, a repair shop, a hospice, or a shelter. Hospitality is a shelter for the soul, a healing for the spirit. Ultimately, this is what we offer when we open our home in the true spirit of hospitality or when we bring our gifts of hospitality outside of our homes to reach others.

Just yesterday I joined three special friends for lunch in one of their homes. At one time or another during our college years, we had all been roommates. We were in the same sorority, we were in each other's weddings, and we laughed at the same type of things—a lot. After several months of heightened concern over the health of one of my family members, this retreat was like a fresh breeze on a warm day. The four of us had a heart connection nurtured through the years, a mutual respect and love for each other, and conversations compelling enough that we could have continued all day.

We sat around a nicely set table with candles flickering—at lunch. (Last time I had candles with my PB&J, well, I just can't remember!) The food was takeout from a nearby café. The dessert was homemade apple cake. It was simple hospitality at its best. Nothing extravagant, just a few lovely touches to make our lunch extra-special. As I departed I was filled with gratitude for lifelong girlfriends. My friend's hospitality was truly a "hospital for my soul."

O—OBEDIENCE

Some may think focusing on hospitality is frivolous or a waste of time. But in reality it is nothing less than obeying God's clear command in Scripture. Hospitality was not Martha Stewart's invention; it was God's! We are to share His love with others. Are we prepared to obey?

We know from the book of Romans that we are to "practice" hospitality. What does that mean exactly? The New Century Version says this: "Share with God's people who need help. Bring strangers in need into your homes" (Romans 12:13). The heart of hospitality is obedience to God's direction.

Romans 12 paints an incredible picture of what it means to truly give our lives to God.

The apostle Paul spends a lot of time talking about the gifts God has given us and how we should use them, but in verses 9–16, he gets right to the heart of hospitality: "Love each other like brothers and sisters" (verse 10 NCV). "Do not be proud, but make friends with those who seem unimportant" (verse 16 NCV). In these selfless acts, we serve not only those in need but Christ Himself. Hospitality is obeying God by cheerfully serving others.

S—SIMPLICITY

There is a certain unencumbered feeling when we have a simple approach to hospitality. It's important enough that this whole book is about simplicity—but why? I believe that if we don't approach hospitality simply, most of us won't do it at all.

Oscar Wilde said, "I adore simple pleasures. They are the last refuge of the complex." When we exchange the harried hoopla for the heartfelt, everyone involved is blessed. The Bible's examples of hospitality are often the simplest. Inviting someone in for a bite to eat. Offering a weary traveler a refreshing drink of water. Hostesses didn't have to dash around cleaning house before anyone could set foot in the door, nor did they run out and purchase the perfect decorations and table accessories. They were comfortable sharing their "real selves" with others.

Perhaps that's the most significant reason for simplicity: being real. Can we be comfortable when everything is not perfect, or do we always need to put on a show for people? I want everything to be just right when guests arrive, but as my aunt always says, "I don't want to buy your house; I just want to visit." Simplicity brings us closer to having authentic relationships. Our focus is on our guests, not on the "stuff" that surrounds us. Simplicity is a vital ingredient in any effective approach to hospitality.

P—PRAYER

Hospitality involves prayer. I like to keep a list of people with whom I'd like to share hospitality, and I pray for them regularly, asking God to show me opportunities to share time with them. I need Him to show me the best time and place to reach out to the people on my list. I don't always know what each individual needs from me, but God does! I've found that when I'm trying to seek God's direction on a specific issue, if I write down my prayers, my focus stays on the issue at hand. Often I feel God leading me to something very simple—a note, a phone call, or meeting somewhere for coffee.

When we're planning to share time with an individual or a group of people, we should also pray for that gathering, asking God to bless the conversation and to be present in all those interactions. We need His divine leading to make the connections He wants us to make and to know how best to minister to others.

Another way to pray is for people you don't know yet. Ask God to show you individuals with whom He wants you to share your hospitality. You might be surprised at who turns up!

I—INTIMACY

An intimate moment adds a special dimension to our overcrowded lives. Intimacy is sharing who you are and what you are with others. A quiet dinner, a meaningful conversation, a kind deed—all are building blocks to closeness. You need this type of relationship with your husband, your family, and your closest friends, but nurturing genuine intimacy takes time and effort.

Time has a way of slipping through our fingers like the sand in an hourglass. In our high-tech society of cell phones, pagers, and instant e-mail, we count minutes while our parents and grandparents counted pennies. We are *so* busy! Rarely do we allow our minds to contemplate taking time to sit quietly with a friend. Uninterrupted conversations and listening hearts are uncommon today and are highly esteemed. Walking in the rain with a child, reading a book to a toddler, and holding the hand of someone before surgery have value beyond price. Crying with a friend and giving a hug encourage and affirm us. Our hearts are uplifted and our spirits are refreshed. Time plus realness plus genuine caring equals intimacy.

Honest intimacy is the capacity to be real with another person. Being authentic with another and offering that person the safety and love to be real with you is the best definition of true hospitality.

To capture intimacy, schedule time one-on-one with a friend, a family member, or an acquaintance you'd like to know better. It's easy these days—"Let's meet for coffee" is more popular than ever! A coffeehouse is wonderful, an intimate tea shop is even better, and often, your own kitchen is best of all. Sometimes intimacy feels awkward at first, but the rewards of a real connection make it all worth it.

T—TO GO

Do you have a plan for exporting your kindness? Having a stockpile of ideas will make the process of taking your hospitality on the road a smooth and successful venture. It removes the guesswork from the God work!

My friend Holly is an expert at this. She has a stack of recipes that are simple to prepare, and she tries to keep the ingredients on hand so that she can prepare a meal or a welcoming treat for someone in need. In fact, just the other day I was a thankful recipient of her hospitality-to-go plan.

My mother had been in the hospital for weeks, a new year of school had just begun, and my work load was stacking up. Holly called to say that she and Susan (my walking friends) wanted to bring over dinner. I said in my most polite manner, "Oh, we're fine, but thank you for your thoughtfulness." I was lying, of course; I knew at that moment groceries were nowhere to be found in our home. That evening after my daughter and I arrived home from the hospital, the doorbell rang. It was Holly with a taco casserole, bread, fruit salad, and cookies. She and Susan had worked together to create this meal and ease the pressure I was feeling. There is something extra-special about busy people who take time to reach out and help others. As you read through the pages of this book, make notes of the ideas that strike you so that you can create your own signature style of offering hospitality to go.

A—ACKNOWLEDGE AND APPRECIATE

We all have our own gifts, but those who are known for being hospitable need a "dose of their own medicine" once in a while. They need to be acknowledged for their kindness, appreciated for their efforts, and recipients of the hospitality of others. Why not you?

After a speaking engagement on the topic of hospitality, a lady came to visit with me. She was a minister in the church that was hosting the women's event. She explained to me that her spiritual gift was hospitality. As we talked, she shared that very seldom does anyone extend the courtesy of hospitality to her. She asked me, "Would you please add to your talk the importance of reaching out to others who reach out all the time?"

I asked, "Do you intimidate others with unattainable acts of kindness?" She didn't think so. As we talked, I realized that most of us are "takers" by nature, and unless we make a conscious effort, we'll always take and forget to give back. Those who are more "givers," either by nature or intent, often get taken for granted.

It made me think: who do I need to give to, and who do I frequently take from? It was a good conversation to help spawn a new way of thinking about how we use our gifts within the body of Christ. I prayed for this lady in hopes that someone would reach out to her so she would feel acknowledged and appreciated. In our busy lives, gratitude is often felt yet not expressed. So as we think about those who need our hospitality, let's not overlook those who've been offering it to us.

L—LIFESTYLE

Hospitality is a lifestyle, a ministry lifestyle. We each have ministries that God weaves into our hearts. We all need each other to make the body of Christ its best. When you make hospitality your ministry, you're making the commitment to a lifestyle of opening up your heart to others on a regular basis.

Creating a hospitable lifestyle starts small, perhaps by committing to one intentional act of hospitality each month. Gradually as you see how easy and rewarding hospitality can be, you might increase to one per week. Eventually, you'll be starting each day asking God, "How can I reach out to someone today?" and it will have truly become your lifestyle.

Think for a moment how God might use you today, this week, or this month. Creating a ministry lifestyle is allowing God to work through us, and when He is working through us, we cannot fail—we just know we are here on earth doing all we can to bring glory to Him and others to the kingdom.

I—IDEAS

Stock up on the best, brightest, and most doable ideas for hospitality. Develop a radar for them. Scan your favorite magazines. Talk with your friends. You may even want to keep a simple notebook or card file with your favorite recipes, holiday decorating ideas, party themes, and anything else that spurs your hospitality thinking. This book is packed full of ideas to help make sharing with others easy and fun.

When I'm trying to get my imagination going, I like to look at an object and think of five ways to use it creatively in hospitality—it might be as a decoration or as a gift. As an example, you might have a medium-sized trunk in your basement and you haven't decided what to do with it. Here are some thoughts:

- Set the trunk at one end of a buffet table—use it to hold plates, napkins, and silverware.
- Place potted mums and English ivy in the trunk and set it on the front porch.
- Fill it with inexpensive dress-up clothes and hats. Give it as a gift to a young niece.
- Place it on your fireplace hearth and use it to hold magazines—or favorite seasonal books.
- Place it on top of your refrigerator for decoration.

T—TIME

I could write an entire book on the subject of time. We never have enough of it, do we? That's why hospitality is such a valuable gift to others. It means we gave them our most precious resource: our time.

Because time is so limited, it's even more important to keep hospitality simple. We use our time wisely when we find ways to incorporate hospitality into things we're already doing. Perhaps you're making a casserole for dinner—would it be just as easy to double the recipe and share with someone in need? Perhaps you've made snickerdoodles for the bake sale and you have a few extra—why not invite a neighbor for an afternoon break of coffee and cookies? If you're heading to the market for your weekly shopping, do you know a new mom who could use a few groceries?

If your time is limited, begin your quest to practice hospitality in these small ways. I bet it will be so rewarding that soon you'll find yourself wanting to create more time in your schedule to plan more acts of kindness!

Y—YOU

Are you taking care of yourself so that you are equipped to take care of others? In order to choose a lifestyle of hospitality, you must first love yourself so you are capable of loving others.

In chapter 1, we discussed the spring-cleaning aspects of assessing our existence. When we've taken the time to put our own hearts in order, we are freed to reach beyond ourselves to meet others where they are.

Author Shirley Kane Lewis puts it this way: "To live life to the fullest, we need to embrace the values inherent in hospitality. To do this, we first need to be hospitable to ourselves. I equate hospitality with being compassionate, caring and giving to ourselves. It is treating ourselves kindly, without judgment or self-deprecation. When we do this, all the rest will follow."[1]

SIMPLE SOLUTIONS

Gracious hospitality involves four simple steps:
1. You comfort others.
2. You encourage others.
3. You forgive others.
4. You give to others.

CHAPTER THREE

Homeland Hospitality

Every house where love abides and friendship is a guest
Is surely home, and home, sweet home
For there the heart can rest.

—Henry Van Dyke

What image comes to mind when you hear the word *home*? As I reflect on bits and pieces of my life, I repeatedly focus fondly on the homes I have lived in, from those of my childhood to the one sheltering me now. The dictionary defines *home* as one's residence, but to me the word *home* means so much more. In school, students are grouped by homeroom. In business, employees obtain information from the home office. While cooking, we prefer homegrown fruits and vegetables. In baseball, you are safe when you reach home plate. Home should be a place for receiving what you need—relaxation, rejuvenation, and restoration.

Women set the tone of the home. We are in the business of growing hearts while preventing damage from the weeds the world blows into our garden. The responsibility can be overwhelming at times, but we are God's chosen people for this extraordinary task. I desperately want my home to be a safe haven, a retreat, a space to regroup, and a loving place to repair the damage the world throws our way. Our houses, whether large or small, offer only walls and a roof. A home is created inside when we use our imaginations to create a space that nurtures souls. When our four walls adopt our personality, they become a perfect place to share ourselves. I want my home to have a welcoming environment that showers the spirit of hospitality on all who enter.

The best houses "come from the heart," and are created by people who know who they are and express it.

—CHARLOTTE MOSS

As believers in God, we have three homes: our earthly home, our church home, and our heavenly home. Each of our homes should be a place of grace where we can let our hair down and just be ourselves.

OUR EARTHLY HOME

According to Karen Mains, author of *Open Heart, Open Home*, "Hospitality, like charity, must begin at home. We need to make a point to say, 'It's so good to have you home,' or those other words, 'It's so good to come home to you.' Our homes should be filled with gentle considerations, cherishing, openness and love."[1]

Hospitality not only starts at home, but it truly begins with us. We must offer hospitality to ourselves before we can offer it to our family, our friends, and our community. This sounds lovely, but how does it go into practice? By knowing and living our priorities, seeking God's direction daily, taking good care of our health, focusing on kindness, sharing transparently, and loving unconditionally.

SIX STEPS TO HONING HOSPITALITY AT HOME

1. KNOW AND LIVE YOUR PRIORITIES
2. SEEK GOD'S DIRECTION DAILY
3. TAKE GOOD CARE OF YOUR HEALTH
4. FOCUS ON KINDNESS
5. SHARE TRANSPARENTLY
6. LOVE UNCONDITIONALLY

Take a minute to review your current personal situation. Do you regularly offer *yourself* hospitality? What does that mean?

If hospitality comes down to love and kindness, one of the ways we are kind to ourselves is by doing our best to stay healthy. Do you need to make an annual doctor's appointment? How are your eating habits these days? Are you exercising regularly? If you're like most women, you probably don't sleep enough. Do you need to start getting to bed earlier? We have too much to lose by not being our best selves. Be kind to yourself so you have the energy to be kind to others.

> *The best relationships . . . are built up like a fine lacquer finish,*
> *with accumulated layers made of many little acts of love.*
> —ALAN McGINNIS, *The Friendship Factor*

Next, our hospitality moves from ourselves to our families. Is the air in your home clear of bitterness, resentment, and strife? Do you feel a sense of calm in the midst of a harried world? Keep in mind that home sometimes can be the hardest place to extend hospitable kindnesses. We often are our worst selves at home; we're tired, overworked, and grumpy. When we let down our hair, it has lots of tangles! Our goal is to freely give love and kindness to others, and our starting point is at home.

One effective way to increase harmony at home is by having a regular family meeting. (Be sure to have good snacks, but do not do this during a meal.) Put the issues on the table—communication is the key! Work together to resolve things. Plan together to serve. Spending positive time together, listening to one another's concerns and desires, is the glue that bonds relationships at home. And the bonds with our families last for generations.

My friend Marie has a big family, so every Sunday evening she and her husband hold a family meeting. Attendance is mandatory. This is their weekly air freshener, God style. A big bowl filled with questions pertaining to family issues is placed in the center of their round table, and each family member has a turn to answer a question. Each person shares an affirmation about another family member. Next on the loosely created agenda is what they have scheduled for the next week. They continue by discussing any concerns or trials and conclude with a short devotion and prayer. Connection, communication, and a consistent system of checks and balances allow this family to reinforce the teamwork approach every family strives to achieve.

Our family matters. We should always put people above things and their needs above our convenience. Ask God for a servant's heart. True homeland hospitality begins with an attitude that catapults into action. To best develop this spiritual gift, we start with Scripture. As we bring our gifts and hospitality into loving commitment to God, who Himself reached out to us in love and welcome, our gifts and efforts will be for His glory.

WHAT DOES THE BIBLE SAY ABOUT HOSPITALITY?

- "Share with God's people who are in need. Practice hospitality" (Romans 12:13).
- "Offer hospitality to one another without grumbling" (1 Peter 4:9).
- "Do not forget to entertain strangers, for by so doing some people have entertained angels without knowing it" (Hebrews 13:2).

OUR FRIENDS

For many of us, our friends are like our extended family. We couldn't imagine life without them. Sometimes friends are so "close to home" that we forget to offer them our hospitality. A deep, heart-to-heart talk with a cherished friend feels as comforting and soothing as a supersoft, oversized sweatshirt on a chilly fall day.

Friends are important. A good friend is one who understands your world, difficulties, and triumphs. Thinking of my favorite friends always makes me smile because of all the love, laughter, tears, prayers, and cherished moments. Often our get-togethers revolve around food. We meet at restaurants, at each other's homes for dinner, or at a yogurt shop for a treat. Life would lose its richness without the opportunity to live it with friends. Have you scheduled time with friends lately?

Most of my friends have an over-the-top sense of humor. We spend the majority of our time laughing at something, whether it's a college prank or a funny near disaster at a child's party. Friends who enjoy a long history can pick up where they left off and never miss a beat. They offer joy, share the burdens, and lighten the load.

Currently, I can think of several friends I need to contact, just to tell them they are loved. What about you? If you're like most of us, you probably never get to spend enough time nurturing your meaningful girlfriend relationships. Make a commitment today to call, send an e-mail, write a note, or run by your girlfriend's home or workplace with a small, special treat.

Because it's sometimes hard to keep my girlfriends at the top of my priority list, I like to occasionally create a "just because" gift basket. This is truly a way to extend hospitality to your closest friends. Here are some of my favorite ideas:

SIX EASY FRIENDSHIP BASKETS

Barbecue Basket: Line a basket with a red-and-white tablecloth. Fill with plastic corn-on-the-cob holders, a petite citronella candle, red and white napkins, a long-handled barbecue brush, your favorite sauces, your best picnic recipe, bug repellent, and red or blue plastic cups and plates.

Beach Basket: Line a basket with a beach towel. Fill the basket with suntan oil, a beach ball, a shovel and pail, moist hand wipes, flip-flops, and a Beach Boys tape.

Relaxation Basket: Line a basket with a soft floral bath towel. Fill the basket with fragrant votive candles (try getting the same fragrance as the flowers on your bath towel), and add a container of bath salts, bath oils, moisturizers, and a CD or tape of classical music.

Garden Variety Basket: Line a basket with small plastic bags. Fill the basket with small gardening tools, bug repellent, gardening gloves, a straw hat, suntan lotion, bulbs, and a six-pack of your friend's favorite bedding plants.

Kids' Fun Basket: Line a basket with the comics section of the newspaper. Fill the basket with silly putty, face paints, a jar full of lacing beads and string, a funny movie, microwave popcorn, M&Ms, washable paints and sponges, paint smocks, and crazy straws.

Favorites Basket: Line a basket with colorful tissue paper. Fill the basket with your favorite things: favorite candy, fruit, a gift certificate for a favorite music store, a favorite book, and a gift coupon to your favorite ice-cream store.

SIMPLE SOLUTIONS

1. Leave notes in unexpected spots, such as on a pillow, in a lunchbox, on a car window, etc.
2. Look into your loved ones' eyes, smile, and listen.
3. Give big hugs often. I strive for a minimum of eight hugs a day.
4. Have humor breaks that involve everyone.
5. Take time to talk.
6. Share simple hospitality with your friends and family.

OUR CHURCH HOME

Hospitality at church is not just the ever-popular covered-dish dinner or the annual women's tea. Church-related hospitality involves the spiritual nurturing we experience when we join with other believers to worship our Lord. Our church is made up of people who will bear our burdens, lift us in prayer, and be at our side when life is hard.

People need each other. Just one month ago, my mother fell and shattered her hip. It was and will continue to be a difficult experience. On the day she was scheduled for reconstructive surgery, she was in an enormous amount of pain. As we waited for the surgeon to arrive, members from my parents' church began to come into her hospital room. There was laughter amid the pain. These believers came to offer encouragement, prayer support, and kindness. As the orderly prepared to roll Mom out of her hospital room down for surgery, he smiled broadly and said to me, "You can just *feel* the love in this room." He was right. He experienced the power of community among Christians. Genuine hospitality glistens and will help us achieve the goals of becoming more effective in our evangelism and building up one another in the body of Christ.

The church offers God's encouragement through His people, making this an environment we need to choose not for what we can get but for what we can give. Hebrews 10:24–25 says, "Let us think about each other and help each other to show love and do good deeds. You should not stay away from the church meetings, as some are doing, but you should meet together and encourage each other" (NCV).

WHY CHOOSE CHURCH?

- TO HELP EACH OTHER
- TO SHOW LOVE
- TO DO GOOD DEEDS
- TO MEET TOGETHER
- TO ENCOURAGE EACH OTHER

OUR HEAVENLY HOME

In the fourteenth chapter of John, Jesus tells us that He is going to prepare a place for us, a place where we can be with Him. Many think this place is a perfect world in which believers live forever.

The most hospitable thing we can do for others is to share the message of salvation so everyone we meet might hear the good news and pray to make their eternal reservation with God. Jesus already did all the work by coming to this world and dying on a cross so that we may choose eternal life. All He requires of us is the asking. "God loved the world so much that he gave his one and only Son so that whoever believes in him may not be lost, but have eternal life" (John 3:16 NCV).

Can we fathom what incredible things we'll see when we pass through the gates of heaven? Scripture says heaven has streets of gold, flowing crystal waters, and mansions of glory. Talk about a designer showcase—this is the original! Streets of gold, radiant angels, ongoing choruses of praise, a real paradise for the choosing. Imagine the relief of no earthly pain, no stress, no weekly grocery shopping, and no evil to endure. Imagine having a face-to-face conversation with Jesus. What about finding and hugging our loved ones who arrived earlier? Consider hearing the words, "Well done, good and faithful servant!" (Matthew 25:21). The possibilities are mind-boggling. This is God's heavenly hospitality to us. He invites us into heaven, and He has everything ready for us.

CHAPTER FOUR

Beyond Harried Holidays

Hospitality makes for infectious fun.

—ANONYMOUS

Last Christmas was a colossal disaster. I thought I was prepared, but suddenly it became painfully obvious how mistaken I was. December was promotion time for a new book. That means I pack a bunch of boxes full of Christmas pretties and fly around the country to play show and tell for morning television. If this sounds glamorous, stay tuned!

Since I am the pivotal person in our family for making holiday plans, Christmas is no time to be traveling for business. After all, who do you think gets those groceries for the big spread? Who purchases the cinnamon-scented candles? Who makes sure we don't run out of red wrapping paper? Each year I break out in hives when the Christmas carols start wafting through the supermarket. But this year took the fruitcake.

My first media tour destination was Winnipeg, Canada. Thus began my blitz of the Northern frozen tundra, just a few short hours ahead of a nasty blizzard. This was the first twenty-four hours of an eleven-day event taking me from unplanned destination to unplanned destination, crisscrossing America. It truly was a plane, train, bus, and automobile experience. From a jet slipping off the runway in Pittsburgh, to standing in front of a snowdrift twice my height in Chicago . . . if my family had not been coming to meet me in Toronto at the end of the first week, I would have started walking toward my home in Texas. To say the least, my Christmas spirit was dampened.

When the holidays roll around, everything else doesn't automatically stop. We still have work, family, church, and school obligations—sometimes more than ever. Decking the halls may be the last thing on your mind; in fact, anybody who irritates me may be decked himself. Have you ever felt this way? Hopelessly harried? Juggling work responsibilities, cookie baking, and gift shopping while keeping an eye on a depleting bank account? It's time to take a deep breath. Pour a cup of spiced tea. Sit. Rest awhile.

RADICAL RELIEF

There is absolutely no way any woman can possibly do everything expected of her during the holidays, whether it's Christmas, Thanksgiving, or Easter. Just accept it: you can't do everything the holidays demand. There is no reason to feel guilty about choosing a few doable tasks and skipping the others. I want to help you lighten your load.

Prior to the Christmas season, I picture a quaint Norman Rockwell portrait of the family huddled around the holiday table, dressed in seasonal regalia, truly enjoying the moment. *Then I snap out of it.* This just doesn't happen by itself. Holiday happiness takes a positive attitude, smart planning, proper punting, lots of work, and the ability to delegate.

When you find yourself winter weary, or when your best plans blow up in your glitter-laden face, it's time to regroup.

GET A HANDLE ON THE HARRIED HUSTLE

Review your past holidays. What were the Grinch-causing issues? Make a list of all the holiday activities that are typically on your list. Cross out things you do out of guilt or obligation. Pare down your list to only the things that fit your family and truly serve others.

Here are a few more ideas that will help you get a handle on the harried holiday hustle:

- If a few relatives have the power to steal your holiday cheer, mentally prepare yourself ahead of time and ask the Lord's help in not allowing these people to get to you. Make specific plans for how to deal with them—even planning gentle responses to expected irritating comments.

- Should your children covet the entire inventory of Toys "R" Us, help them make a list of their top three favorites. You may also want to take them shopping to choose some gifts to donate to charities. Let them choose, and talk with them about the importance of helping others.

- No time for baking from scratch? Use frozen breads and slice-and-bake cookies (add your own special glaze for a homemade touch), and let the local grocery store bake your pies. You can still serve them beautifully displayed on Grandma's favorite pie plate.

- If gift giving is getting your goat this year, simplify by making coupons for baby-sitting in January, a cake of their choice delivered sometime in February, or a picnic lunch in March.

- Last year's black velvet party pants too tight? Call some resale shops in your area, sell your old pair, and buy a new pair that makes you feel great!

Now take another deep, cleansing breath of the air God created. As we approach the holiday season, we should do so with an eternal perspective.

Here are more simple ideas to choose from as you deck your halls and hit the malls.

THE TWELVE DOUGHS OF CHRISTMAS

Mix and match your Christmas cookies. Start with a terrific sugar-cookie dough—then let your imagination soar! Use refrigerated premade dough or a boxed sugar-cookie mix. Then add one of the following mix-ins:

$\frac{1}{2}$ cup cranberries and $\frac{1}{2}$ cup white chocolate chips
$\frac{1}{2}$ cup chocolate chips and $\frac{1}{2}$ cup crushed toffee bars
$\frac{1}{2}$ cup red and $\frac{1}{2}$ cup green cherries, chopped
$\frac{1}{2}$ cup fresh mint leaves, chopped
$\frac{1}{2}$ cup pistachios, chopped, and $\frac{1}{4}$ cup
    fresh cranberries, chopped

1 cup of red and green M&Ms combined

$\frac{1}{2}$ cup candied ginger, chopped

1 cup cinnamon red hots

1 cup mint chocolate chips

$\frac{1}{2}$ cup macadamia nuts, chopped, and $\frac{1}{2}$ cup cranberries, chopped

$\frac{1}{2}$ cup candied orange rind, chopped, and 1 cup chocolate chips

Or for easy cinnamon pinwheels, roll out the dough on a floured surface and sprinkle with swirls of $\frac{1}{4}$ cup cinnamon and $\frac{1}{4}$ cup nutmeg. Roll up the dough like a jelly roll, slice, and bake.

HAUTE COCOA

Last-minute gifts can be ready and waiting with cocoa to go. This inexpensive and simply packaged idea can be made ahead and tucked away for a delicious treat for the entire family. Get creative with your favorite spices or imported chocolate to create your own signature cocoa. This recipe makes enough for five gifts.

6 cups unsweetened cocoa

2 cups malted milk powder

7 cups granulated sugar

2 tablespoons cinnamon

1 teaspoon cardamom

1 vanilla bean, split in half

zest of one orange (optional)

Blend all ingredients and let sit for three days. Spoon into five gift jars. (Simple Ball canning jars are available at most supermarkets and look lovely with a ribbon tied around the top.) Include these instructions with your gift: *Mix $\frac{1}{4}$ cup of mix into an 8- to 10-ounce mug of hot milk.*

WINTER WONDERLAND

When creating an atmosphere in your home, start with the senses of sight and smell. A fresh bough of greenery, cinnamon sticks simmering in apple juice on the stove, a fragrant votive flickering in a small crystal bowl—these quick touches leave a big impression. Here are some other simple ideas for bringing that holiday feeling to your home.

SEVEN WAYS TO CREATE A REAL HOLIDAY HAVEN

1. Purchase a petite Christmas tree for each bedroom in your home. Decorate the trees to coordinate with the style and color of each room.
2. Place a basket of seasonal goodies close to your front door. Candy canes, mini gingerbread loaves, and small jars of homemade cranberry sauce are some ideas. Give these to your guests as they leave your home.
3. Save all of your children's Christmas books. Place them in baskets around the house, especially in front of the fireplace and Christmas tree.
4. Sprinkle Christmas confetti everywhere: on your tablecloth, on the packages under the tree, and inside your Christmas cards and letters.
5. Affix a fresh evergreen garland around each doorframe in your home. Hang candy canes, pine cones, and ribbons on the garland.
6. Wrap your entry doors like large presents. Use six-inch ribbon down the middle and make a huge bow for the center. Spotlight the outside doors.
7. When entertaining during the Christmas season, encourage guests to mingle throughout your home. Create a roving buffet by setting up Christmas candies, bowls of punch, eggnog, and coffee in the living room, dining room, kitchen, family room, and study. Your friends and family will be able to enjoy your holiday decorations while exploring your home.

SIX TANTALIZING TREE TRIMMINGS

1. Beary Merry Christmas: Gather stuffed bears of all sizes and colors. Select a ribbon color that will coordinate with your gift-wrap and use it to tie big ribbons around each bear's neck. On the back of the ribbon stick a little ornament hanger and hang the bow-tied bears all over the tree.

2. Twelve Days of Christmas: Make small copies of the musical score to "The Twelve Days of Christmas." Start decorating the tree with the classic song. Fill in the empty areas with partridges, pear trees, drums, gold rings, two turtledoves, four calling birds, and a few French hens. (You can often find these small décor items at dollar stores.)

3. Stocking Tree: Stockings old and new, borrowed and blue make this tree a step above. Collect stockings from tag sales, Christmas stores, and attics. Purchase some gold cording and tie the stockings to the tree.

4. Adoring Angels: Angels of all shapes and sizes grace the branches of this Christmas tree. Wrap star garland around the tree and then fill in the spaces with angels. Tuck in several shiny halos and sprinkle with angel dust for a heavenly touch.

5. We Three Kings: Frame the bottom of this tree with a large purple robe fit for a king. Decorate the tree with mini crowns (found at most craft stores). Make a garland of star shapes and shiny beads to represent the star the wise men followed in search of baby Jesus.

6. Helping-Hand Mittens: This tree is a burst of color. Make salt-dough ornaments by using a hand-shaped cookie cutter. (See recipe below). Purchase several pairs of colorful mittens. After making the hand ornaments, paint the nails and accessorize with shiny jewel "rings." Tie the decorated hand ornaments to the tree with coordinating ribbons. Place colorful mittens in between the hands for extra color.

SALT-DOUGH ORNAMENTS

2 cups flour
1 cup salt
1 cup water

Mix salt and flour. Add in half the water, then gradually add the remaining water. Knead until the dough is smooth. (This can take up to ten minutes). For flat dough ornaments, roll out the dough on baking paper. You can also be creative and make odd shapes and wreaths. (These take longer to bake.) Use cookie cutters, cutout templates, or just your hands. Dust dough with flour and begin to add details to the ornaments with a toothpick, Popsicle stick, and knife.

SIMPLE SOLUTIONS AT CHRISTMAS

1. Christmas cards can be simplified by sending an e-mail card, with some of the year's pictures attached, to your family and friends (no stamps)!
2. Buy tape, gift cards, and wrapping paper in bulk. Store them in a big plastic box with a pair of scissors.
3. Fill a bowl with scented pine cones to use as a lovely tabletop centerpiece.
4. Create a holiday binder and fill it with recipes, Christmas card lists, a list of gifts given the previous year, and hints for where you hid those gifts you bought early.
5. Start using your Christmas china on December 1. Don't have special place settings? Buy decorative holiday paper napkins—they make each meal seem more special!

THANKSGIVING

Thanksgiving is my favorite holiday. I love the cooler temperatures, crisp leaves, and porches lined with pumpkins. Coming from a family in which food plays a big role in any get-together, I can close my eyes and smell the celery simmering in real butter for the cornbread dressing and the yeast wafting through the kitchen as the rolls rise for the second time.

Thankfulness, gratitude, and blessings are the cornerstones of hospitality, especially at Thanksgiving. My friend Ellie Kay asks each year for friends and family around the country to send her a leaf-shaped note with their family's greatest blessing or answered prayer of the past year. She makes a construction paper tree trunk, affixes it to a wall in her home, and attaches the leaves to the trunk. As her family enjoys the season, they reflect on the blessings they and their friends have shared all year long.

What are you thankful for, and how does your family share their gratitude during this wonderful time of year?

The Thanksgiving season is a perfect time to show people that you appreciate them. Here are a few simple recipe ideas perfect for gift giving. A small gift at Thanksgiving usually surprises people, showing them how much you care!

CRANBERRY-APPLE CHUTNEY

2 cups fresh cranberries
1 cup Granny Smith apples, peeled and chopped
2/3 cup orange juice
1/2 cup sugar
1 teaspoon lemon rind
1 tablespoon crystallized ginger

Place all ingredients in a two-quart saucepan. Bring to a boil. Reduce heat to low. Cover and simmer until cranberries pop and mixture thickens slightly. Store in refrigerator.

PUMPKIN PIE CAKE

1 29-ounce can pumpkin

4 eggs

1 13-ounce can evaporated milk

1 cup sugar

$\frac{1}{2}$ cup brown sugar

$\frac{1}{4}$ teaspoon salt

$1\frac{1}{2}$ teaspoons vanilla

2 teaspoons cinnamon

$\frac{1}{2}$ teaspoon pumpkin pie spice

1 box spice cake mix (can substitute yellow or white)

2 sticks melted butter

1 cup chopped pecans

Preheat oven to 350 degrees. Mix the first nine ingredients. Spread in a 9 x 13 inch pan. Sprinkle cake mix over the mixture. Pour butter over the cake mix. Sprinkle with chopped pecans. Bake for one hour at 350 degrees.

SIMPLE SOLUTIONS AT THANKSGIVING

1. Entertaining the entire family is not simple, but it can be! Delegate. You supply the home and meat; ask everyone else to bring their favorite and enjoy the buffet.
2. Small pumpkins and silly-shaped squash also make great place cards for your Thanksgiving table.

EASTER

Easter is a joyous time when we remember that Jesus Christ came back to life after paying the penalty for our sins. Easter also is a gorgeous time of year—buds on the trees, nurseries blooming with vibrant colors, and lots and lots of eggs!

Easter makes me think of honey-glazed hams, deviled eggs, and large bowls of potato salad atop a freshly pressed tablecloth. I remember white straw hats, white sandals, and goose bumps on my arms, because the weather was not quite warm enough for my sleeveless, wispy chiffon dress. Pastel-colored baskets full of candy, bunnies, and books make Easter a time to look forward to sharing with family and friends.

Here are some simple ideas for making Easter special:

- Go on a tree branch hunt. Find a sturdy branch that will fit in a tall glass cylinder. Hot-glue ribbon to the top of colorful plastic eggs. Hang these on the branch to make an egg tree.
- Dye eggs and place them in a crystal bowl to add color to your dining room, entry, or Easter baskets.

RUBBER BAND–DYED EGGS

You will need:

Eggs

Saucepan

Water

Newspaper

Rubber bands of different widths

Egg dye

Bowl

Large spoon

Paper towels

Instructions:

1. Boil the eggs for thirteen minutes.
2. Run the eggs under cold water until they are cool.
3. Spread newspapers on your worktable.
4. Wind rubber bands around the hard-boiled eggs in various directions. Be sure to leave spaces between the rubber bands.

5. Put the egg dye in a bowl and mix it with water, following the dye directions.

6. Keep the eggs in the dye until they have reached your favorite shade.

7. Lift the eggs from the dye and place them on newspaper to dry. When dry, remove the rubber bands.

8. Try using natural dyes: coffee, cranberry juice, beets, onion skins, blueberry juice, and red cabbage.

Deviled eggs are often an Easter special. Try this idea to create a different twist to the egg: instead of putting your boiled egg on its side to cut in half lengthwise, sit it up straight, cut a slice off the narrow end and save, hollow out the egg, and prepare according to your regular recipe. Restuff the egg and set the saved portion of the cooked white to use as a little hat atop the stuffed egg.

As Easter is an opportunity for new beginnings, approach this season with prayer, soul-searching, and freshness. I use this time to redo my flowerpots, put out new ferns, and refresh our home from winter into spring. It is a time to enjoy God's grace and goodness in sending His Son to address our iniquities. Take this time to praise Him, worship Him, and tell others of His love.

In her book *Family Celebrations at Easter*, Ann Hibbard suggests, "Shoot the gospel straight with your children, speak on their terms, seek God together as a family. . . . A heart that is open to God will soon be filled with a joy that spills over into the lives around it."[1]

BOOKS TO SHARE THE SEASON

EASTER—*MISS FANNIE'S HAT*, BY JAN KARON

THANKSGIVING—*THE PUMPKIN PATCH PARABLE*,
BY LIZ CURTIS HIGGS

CHRISTMAS—*THE TALE OF THREE TREES*,
BY ANGELA ELWELL HUNT

Host a neighborhood egg hunt for the kids. Ask each participating family to fill twenty-five plastic eggs with wrapped candies. Have the husbands show up early to distribute the eggs in the chosen hunting ground. Hunt! Enjoy the opportunity to visit with your neighbors, and invite them to church.

SIMPLE SOLUTIONS AT EASTER

1. A dyed egg with a name written on it makes a wonderful place card for your Easter table.
2. Never underestimate the pleasure of a holiday buffet at your favorite local restaurant. Just make reservations.
3. Having a crowd at Easter? Order out and arrange your bounty in individual baskets on a large table for everyone to pick up and take to a desired location—such as the backyard or front porch—for a picnic Easter lunch.

PART TWO

Home Sweet Home

CHAPTER FIVE

Faking Homemaking

If you do housework for $10 a week, that's domestic service.
If you do it for nothing, that's matrimony.

—ANONYMOUS

Homemaking. The word sounds so simple, so doable, almost serene. Magazines glamorize it, and television advertisements make it seem so easy. But we in the trenches know how dull these ongoing household chores can be. Mr. Webster says a *homemaker* is one who manages a household. There are many days when I feel certain that my household is managing me. Homemaking boils down to a nasty four-letter word: *work*. Do you think Ms. Proverbs 31 had these thoughts? Probably not—since verse 15 tells us that she had servant girls! Sadly, I'm fresh out of servants.

When Mark and I first married, our home-maintenance styles were polar opposites, which, on occasion, offered the setting for downright chilliness. He was a self-proclaimed Mr. Clean with a supposed "right way" to clean everything. I, on the other hand, couldn't grab the phone book fast enough to find the most economical maid service.

I would not go so far as to say I was a slob, but let's just say I was "cleaning challenged." We were both raised during the *Leave It to Beaver* reruns, and Mark bought into that 1950s mind-set, big time. I was a liberated new millennium lady who knew for sure that Mrs. Cleaver was a fantasy. So we had some meeting in the middle to do.

We tried dividing the chores and talking about how we felt. But mostly, Mark cleaned while I felt guilty for not assuming my wifely duties. Slowly, under his tutelage, I have grown to understand the importance of a spic-and-span household. Since

I love entertaining and consider hospitality my ministry, a clean home comes in handy!

I finally realized that to have a home prepared to offer a hospitable environment for guests we need a plan to keep the place presentable. Moving the mountains of mess into manageable tasks is the key.

MOUNTAIN MOVING PLAN

(Let's call this the M&M plan just to add some flavor.)

Now, there is clean and there is clean. The first step in basic home maintenance is deciding what *clean* means to you and your family. Once you have agreed on that, you have the goal you want to consistently reach. To get started, ask yourself and other family members five questions:

1. What are our must-dos, should-dos, and would-be-so-nice-to-dos?
2. What are our time limits to complete certain tasks?
3. What and to whom might I delegate?
4. What task can I completely finish in a short amount of time?
5. How might I reward myself for a job well done? (This is my personal favorite.)

I find comfort in knowing that time management and consistent homemaking are two of the most difficult yet helpful skills a woman can develop. When the to-dos get you down, remember you are not only honing a lifelong skill, but you are also preparing the place for more important heart work.

> *You may touch the dust in this house, but please don't write in it!*
> *If you write in the dust, please don't date it!*
>
> —ANONYMOUS

CLEAN LIVING

With your M&M plan in hand, it's time to learn the proper method of speed cleaning. This next section will take you room by room with a quick, manageable list to help you keep your focus. The keys to avoiding stress here are the same ones that work for life: keep looking to the finish line, and when a task is daunting, review it in the light of eternity. Take a deep breath (not while holding bleach or any cleaning product), and press on. Here we go!

KITCHEN

Start with the sink. As I peer over the laptop this very second, mine is full of dishes. Excuse me a moment—I'll be right back.

Wow, I feel so much better with a clean sink. So does the author of *Sink Reflections*, Marla Cilley, who advises, "Keep it empty and shining." Also the creator of www.FlyLady.net, a housekeeping Web site, Cilley explains, "A sparkling sink becomes your kitchen's benchmark for hygiene and tidiness, inspiring you to load the dishwasher immediately and keep counters, refrigerator doors, and stove top tidy too."[1]

SHINY SINK 101

- Fill sink to the rim with very hot water; add one cup regular bleach. Soak for one hour.
- Drain and rinse thoroughly.
- Scrub with Ajax, Bon Ami, or baking soda.
- Be sure to rinse thoroughly.
- Shine with Windex or another glass-cleaning spray. Dry thoroughly.[2]

Since I'm in the kitchen, I like to start by enjoying a quick cup of caffeine to prime the engine for a fast yet efficient cleaning machine. Then I follow this simple list of quick cleaning tips:

Every day:
Wipe down sink after cleanup—thirty seconds
Wipe down stovetop—one minute
Wipe down countertops—one minute
Sweep or vacuum floor—two minutes

Every week:

Mop the floor—five minutes

Wipe cabinets, backsplashes, and appliances—ten minutes

Wipe switch plates and phone—one minute

Empty and wipe out garbage can—one minute

TIPS FOR ORGANIZING YOUR KITCHEN

1. To organize kitchen cupboards, take everything out of the cupboards and clean out the dust. Before putting items back, line the bottoms of the shelves with contact paper. This will make the shelves easier to clean, especially pantry shelves.

2. Prevent dust buildup and unwanted insects by storing glasses and cups upside down.

3. If possible, leave a lower cupboard stocked with plastic cups, bowls, plates, and utensils just for the kids. This will enable them to help themselves without having to get up into a high cabinet.

4. Store oversized utensils in a crock or pitcher by the stove or on the countertop. For an inexpensive yet tidy look, cover a large coffee can with patterned contact paper to match your kitchen's décor. This is plenty of room for all those big spoons and such.

5. Number lids and bottoms of plastic storage containers with a permanent marker so that they are easy to match up.

6. Make use of the insides of cabinet doors. Tape pieces of paper that have been laminated with info such as kitchen measurements, favorite recipes, or a baby-sitter's phone list.

7. Make a bookshelf for your cookbooks by using an eye-level cupboard shelf. They will be readily available and not gathering dust elsewhere.

BATHROOM

You can clean a bathroom almost as quickly as you can brush your teeth. If it becomes a daily habit, you won't find yourself buried in soap scum or some other nasty bathroom by-product. Think of it as your daily sparkle! Here's how:

Every day:

Wipe out the sink—thirty seconds

Wipe the toilet seat and rim—fifteen seconds

Swish the toilet bowl with a brush—fifteen seconds

Wipe the mirror and faucet—fifteen seconds

Squeegee the shower door—thirty seconds

Spray the shower and curtain with shower mist after every use—fifteen seconds

Every week:

Scrub the tub—three minutes

Scrub the tiles—five minutes

Mop the floor—two minutes

Wipe switch plates, doorknobs, and doorjambs—one minute

Empty and wipe out wastebasket—thirty seconds

TIPS FOR ORGANIZING YOUR BATHROOM

1. After cleaning out your medicine cabinet, attach a magnet strip to the back of the inside. This will hold small metal objects like tweezers, scissors, and nail clippers.
2. Simplify the battle of the towels by color-coding towels and washcloths. Assign a color to each family member. This will stop the fights over whose towel is whose and keep track of who "forgot" to hang up their towels.
3. Keep vanity drawers tidy by using a divided plastic silverware tray. This is great for keeping track of bobby pins, hair elastics, and whatever else will fit inside.
4. Keep a box of disposable gloves under the sink for the inevitable ultra-grimy cleaning tasks.
5. Store bath toys in a dishpan under the vanity (after they have dripped dry). Or hang them in a mesh bag over the shower nozzle.
6. Bath oils or even a regular bath will produce rings around the tub. Taking bubble baths or showers will cut down on these rings.
7. Reduce soap slime by switching to liquid soap in a dispenser for hand washing, or body wash for the shower.

BEDROOM

We may be tempted to hide messy bedrooms behind closed doors, but keeping your bedrooms tidy is essential to creating a relaxing environment for you, your husband, and your kids to sleep. Here are some quick cleaning tips for your bedrooms:

Every day:

Make the bed—two minutes

Fold clothing and put away—four minutes

Straighten the nightstand surfaces—thirty seconds

Every week:

Change the sheets—five minutes

Dust all surfaces—ten minutes

Dust or mop the floors or vacuum the carpet—five minutes

Throw out old magazines—one minute

Wipe switch plates, doorknobs, and doorjambs—one minute

Wipe and disinfect the telephone—thirty seconds

TIPS FOR ORGANIZING YOUR KIDS' ROOMS

1. If you constantly have to combat your kids' writing or drawing on the walls, apply an easy-to-do "wainscoting" using colored or patterned contact paper. Think of it as durable and washable wallpaper. And whenever you get ready to change it, peel it off and start over!

2. It's hard to get kids to clean up their rooms, but make it easier by making sure that there is a place for everything, such as a hamper for the clothes, a bin or toy box for the toys, and a shelf for books and games.

3. Paint a small table and chairs to match the room décor. A child-sized patio table and chairs can be easily decorated with stickers.

4. Use a colorful tackle box for crayons, pencils, and markers. It also travels well!

FAMILY ROOM AND LIVING ROOM

The most used rooms in the house are definitely the messiest! Here are a few helpful tips on keeping your family room and living room presentable:

Every day:

Pick up crumbs and dust bunnies with a handheld vacuum—one minute

Fluff the couch and chair cushions—two minutes

Fold throws after use—thirty seconds

Wipe tabletops and spot-clean cabinets when you see fingerprints—one minute

Straighten coffee-table books and magazines, throw out newspapers, and put away
CDs and videos—two minutes

Every week:

Dust all surfaces, including electronics, books, blinds, picture frames, window sills
and ledges, and tops of doorframes; remove all cobwebs—fifteen minutes

Dust or mop floors or vacuum the rugs and carpet—five minutes

Vacuum the upholstery—five minutes

Throw out old magazines—one minute

Wipe switch plates, doorknobs, and doorjambs—one minute

Wipe and disinfect the phone—thirty seconds

Vacuum the heating and air-conditioning vents—one minute

TIPS FOR ORGANIZING YOUR LIVING ROOM AND FAMILY ROOM

1. Keep in mind that sometimes less is more when it comes to getting rid of clutter in the family room or living room. It will make the room appear larger as well as cleaner.
2. If you have small children, keep an attractive bin or basket with a lid to hold the toys that always seem to clutter the living room.
3. To keep the remote from getting lost, attach it to the side of the TV with a strip of Velcro, or find a decorative box to use as the remote's home.
4. For children who love to sit or lie on the floor, provide some twenty-four-inch square pillows for them to lounge on. They can be stowed away in a corner when not in use.

FAKING IT

It has taken me years to come up with all these housekeeping tips! When Mark and I were first married, I spent all my time pondering all the ways to get out of these tasks. I invented some top-notch fake fixes to make people *think* I was a good home-maker! Here's my list—tongue firmly planted in cheek.

1. Light the oven, throw a teaspoon of cinnamon in a pie pan, turn off the oven, and explain that you have been baking cookies for a bake sale for a favorite charity and haven't had time to clean. It works every time! (Be sure to stock some slice-and-bake cookies in the freezer, sneak those out when no one is looking, and assure your family that you saved some cookies for them.)

2. Chop a large onion, place a couple of tablespoons of olive oil in a sauté skillet, turn the heat to simmer, and cover. This will make the house smell as if dinner is around the corner as you literally round the corner to the market to pick up a prepared feast.

3. Layers of dirty film on windows and screens provide a helpful filter against harmful rays from the sun. Call it an SPF factor of 30 and leave it alone.

4. Cobwebs artfully draped over lampshades reduce the glare from the bulb, thereby creating a romantic atmosphere. If someone points out that the light fixtures need dusting, look confused and exclaim, "What? And spoil the mood?" (During September and October, call it Halloween décor; sprinkle cobwebs with glitter at the holidays to create a unique sparkle of Christmas cheer.)

5. Explain the mounds of pet hair brushed up against the doorways by claiming you are purposely collecting it there to use for stuffing handsewn play animals for underprivileged children. (These mounds of pet hair also keep out cold drafts in winter.)

6. If unexpected company is coming, pile everything unsightly into one room and close the door. As you show your guests through your tidy home, rattle the doorknob to the cluttered room vigorously, fake a growl, and say, "I'd love you to see our den, but Fluffy hates to be disturbed, and the shots are *so* expensive."

7. If time is really crunched and your dust level is out of control, get out your can of Pledge, spray it straight into the air, hit the eye-level spots with a paper towel, and you are good to go.

8. Mix one-quarter cup pine-scented household cleaner with four cups of water in a spray bottle. Mist the air lightly. Leave dampened rags in conspicuous locations. Develop an exhausted look, throw yourself on the couch, and moan, "I clean and I clean and I still don't get anywhere."

9. The bleach swirl is an effective and fast way to dismiss toilet bowl rings. Pour one-half cup of bleach in each toilet in your home; allow it to sit as long as you want the bathroom to smell clean. Run to your neighbors' house if need be and borrow their facilities while in bleach mode.

10. Another favorite, I think from Erma Bombeck: Always keep several get-well cards on the mantel. If unexpected guests arrive, you can say you've been sick and unable to clean.

SIMPLE SOLUTIONS

1. To fluff your pillows, place them in the dryer without heat (just air) for a few minutes. Tumbling removes the dust and fluffs at the same time.
2. Set your timer when cleaning. Clean as fast and furiously as you can, and when the timer dings, take a break.
3. Keep all your cleaning supplies in a bucket. As you move from room to room, you will have everything you need.
4. Wash your kitchen floor right before bed to minimize inconvenience and dirty footprints.
5. Keep vinegar on hand. It works great poured into a bowl to freshen the air and as a rinse to keep floors extra clean.
6. Do a clean sweep of your refrigerator once a week. This will help you avoid growing science experiments a family member might accidentally eat.
7. Clear ammonia works well on glass, stainless steel, chrome, and other shiny surfaces.
8. A super-quick-fix cleaner is ammonia and water—one part ammonia to two parts water.
9. Always keep slice-and-bake cookies in the refrigerator for a quick dessert. You can make them your own by mixing in your family's favorite ingredients.

CHAPTER SIX

Creating a Haven on Earth

*To invite a person to your house is to take charge of his happiness
as long as he is beneath your roof.*

—Jean Anthelme Brillat-Savarin

Our family recently went through the agonizing process of selling our house and moving into an apartment while we look for a new house. For me, the home is an extension of my personality, the nest. For Mark, the home is the cave and does not carry the same sort of emotional attachment. So it was up to me to begin making our new apartment into a "home."

When we express our heart as we decorate our home, we can feel confident about our choices and create a place of comfort. Creating comfort allows us to offer hospitality just by opening the door.

Decorating is a process, and developing the tone or the feeling of your home is the first step. Setting the tone opens the door for color selection, furniture style, and accessory placement. The tone of your home is evident as guests drive up to your personal palace. The front yard, the porch or stoop, and the hallway or entryway are significant spots to consider. As you ponder your space, budget, and family priorities, you begin the process of creating a home that is truly yours.

Redecorating and remodeling take time. Be patient. When redecorating your home, try to finish an entire room before going on to something else. This will give you a sense of accomplishment in seeing a project finished. If you don't, you'll end up with a house full of half-finished projects. It can get discouraging, especially if you want to get everything finished while still adhering to that nasty budget!

I know this from personal experience. In fact, I consider myself an amateur "hummingbird" decorator. I see something I want to change, so I flit over and tackle it—but before I've finished, I feel the need to go on to something else. Soon I'm exhausted with the entire process.

Realizing this approach was not successful, I decided to develop a slower and more intentional approach to redecorating. I began to purchase magazines and start extensive files of things I loved. I collected paint chips from do-it-yourself stores and then developed a plan. At the same time, I spoke with ladies I admire about what approach they took when setting the tone and style of their homes.

MY DECORATING INSPIRATION

Today I went to visit a lady whose home I've admired for years. Her home is gorgeous, appearing effortlessly so. My first question for Karla Kline was, "How do you do this?" Karla began by explaining that she has a very patient family—the type of family who will stop on a whim, knowing that there might be a hidden treasure in that out-of-the-way antique shop.

Karla went on to explain, "I always start backwards. I find something I love and create a room around my treasure." One example of this landed the Kline family a first-place beautification award in a local newspaper. She found a set of weathered antique doors that looked similar to an entrance to an English garden. She put the doors in her garage. The next year she developed a plan to build a stone entrance and path from her side yard to her backyard, with her antique doors showcased between the stone walls. This may not sound simple to you (it didn't to me!), but the concept was a simple one: choose a piece that you love, and take your time creating a space around it.

As we continued our discussion, Karla gave me a tour of her home, offering me a closeup view of her decorating style. Here are a few things I observed:

- Hang pictures low, at eye level for kids, so they can enjoy them too.

- Old bowling pins in a distressed box make a unique item to keep under a sofa table; they also double as a centerpiece for a whimsical event.
- Antique shutters or scuffed-up doors casually leaning against a wall add a unique dimension to a room.
- Weathered window frames, antique ladders, and cement birdbaths look terrific when placed in just the right spot.
- Frame old flags, antique handkerchiefs, or an infant's dedication dress for special accents that showcase family history.

Karla added, "A home is always a work in progress, so if you have a tendency to wait until all is just right, you might be waiting forever." She explained about a time when she hosted a black-tie event for one of her friends who had just been diagnosed with terminal breast cancer. A room was under construction in Karla's house, not even close to being finished, but she moved the construction materials out of the way and had a fancy party in honor of her friend's birthday. Most people would have waited until the work was completed or would have held the party in a different location. But Karla's friend's condition couldn't wait, and Karla knew people wouldn't mind that everything in the house wasn't perfect. The point of hospitality, once again, is focused on love and kindness, not "stuff."

We continued our tour in the dining room. One wall of the room featured a large picture of Karla's oldest son, and she explained that each son would have his picture made at the age of sixteen to be displayed on her dining room wall. Karla's dining room table had been her grandmother's. She cut her very first communion cake on that table, and so have all of her sons. The pictures of her kids, along with the sentimental dining table, set the tone for a true family haven layered with tradition and magnificent memories.

Karla is a decorating inspiration to me because, although her home is more elegant than mine will ever be, her focus is always on creating a space in which her family and friends will feel nurtured. Her focus is on people first, then décor. She has combined style, color, pattern, texture, space, display, and lighting to create a unique place for family living, entertaining, and relaxation.

SEVEN STEPS TO PERSONALIZE YOUR PALACE

1. STYLE
2. COLOR
3. PATTERN
4. TEXTURE
5. SPACE
6. LIGHTING
7. DISPLAY

STYLE

So what about *your* home? If you closed your eyes and imagined exactly what would make your home a retreat for you and your family, where would you start? Deciding on the style that is appropriate for the room, pleasing to your taste, and within your budget is a delicate balance. You must give careful consideration to this important aspect right from the beginning, because your personal style is not something that can be easily or inexpensively changed on a whim.

Style acts like your compass, charting your design direction. What is your style: romantic, adventurous, contemporary, traditional, serene, eclectic, or shabby chic? If you have no idea what your personal style might be, take your time in defining it. Look at magazines and other people's homes for ideas. Look around your own home—what does it say about you?

COLOR

When you have settled on your style, the next big consideration is *color*. Color has a profound influence on the atmosphere of any room, but with the endless array of papers, paints, and fabrics to choose from, it's a subject that can blow you right out of the water! Not to mention the faux finishes, texturing, ragging, and who-knows-what-else.

As Mark and I began deciding on a color scheme for our new home, I wanted to make sure everything flowed. Our home has a very open floor plan, with a large living area that opens into the entry, dining room, breakfast room, and kitchen.

Fortunately for us, we live near a Home Depot, and a friend from church is an interior designer willing to give a few free tips. So I gathered paint chips and finishing techniques until I was blue in the face (just to use a color analogy).

My next color step had more to do with texture and style, which in turn helped us decide our colors. I went to the Dallas Design Center to choose wallpaper. Once again, the choices were abundant. After viewing sample upon sample, I finally found a paper for our dining room that I loved. But what about the price of my beloved wallpaper? Those design showrooms work like a fancy restaurant: they don't print the prices on their samples! There you are, in love with something you cannot afford—which is exactly what happened. By the grace of God, my friend Carol, a general contractor, came to the rescue with a great idea that would allow us to use the expensive wallpaper Mark and I both loved. We put up picture-frame molding and wallpapered the insides of the frames. This gave us the desired effect without the expense of papering the entire dining area. The dining room is very formal now, but it spills out into a great room that is much more family friendly. Because the color scheme is coordinated, the design works.

PATTERN

After you have chosen your style and color, then you need to consider your patterns. When you choose patterns, consider not only their popularity right now but their potential for still looking good ten years from now. This is an important consideration if you're trying to avoid having to redecorate too soon, especially if you're not planning to stay in your house forever. What about the resale appeal?

Resale appeal makes me nuts because it limits your ability to fully make your home your own. However, if you want to be fiscally responsible, you must consider the resale appeal. Everyone remembers the shag carpet that screamed '80s. Or the beads in the doorway that said '70s. Fortunately for you, if you wait thirty years to sell your home, the same styles might have recycled back in vogue! However, if you plan to move before then, choose your patterns carefully with both the present and future in mind.

TEXTURE

Soft velvet, intricate lace, or smooth corduroy—the texture of your furniture, pillows, and lampshades counts in the overall feel of a room. Don't underestimate the significance of texture in your decorating scheme. Without using light and shadow on a variety of surfaces, an otherwise stunning room can appear dull and lifeless. The textural qualities of different fabrics vary, as can be seen if you compare the effect of sunlight shining on the surfaces of silk, cotton, and velvet. Which textures spell comfort to you?

SPACE

So far we've looked at your style, color, pattern, and texture. The next issue at hand is your *space*. Whatever the size of your home, you will want to make the most of your space. Whether you're arranging your things in a new home or rearranging your existing home to maximize your space, it helps to start with an accurate floor plan. That's right—on paper! You might come up with more efficient or creative ways to arrange your furniture if you plot it out on paper first. This comes easy for the left-brained types; however, it's a bit bothersome for us right-brain types. (You could also use one of several great Web sites to help you arrange your rooms, such as the Better Homes and Gardens Web site: www.bhg.com.)

Start by measuring your room, your furniture, and your ceiling height. Then measure any architectural details in the room, such as the fireplace, windows, and doors. Draw a rough sketch of your area that shows the general shape of the room and enter the measurements on the sketch. This paper will be valuable to take along as you select furniture, pictures, lamps, and other accessories, or as you figure out where to place your existing ones. Decide where your seating areas will be, then work out other activities your room will be used for. Do you plan to use the room for work or study? Should it be childproofed with space for high-spirited fun and games? Do you need shelf space for books and treasures? Will there be a television in the room? Do you need good daylight for reading or painting? These are some basic thoughts to consider when arranging your home for sharing hospitality.

LIGHTING

Let there be *light*. Lighting helps create cozy spots or bright work areas. From floor lamps to awesome chandeliers, lighting is an incredible accessory. Once you've thought through your space, you can concentrate on lighting your room. One of the best ways to increase the sense of light in a room is to use only white or pale colors throughout. This works best when a room already has a good amount of natural light.

Concentrate on giving the room warmth and character with splashes of color, and use mirrors to increase the illusion of space and light.

DISPLAY

Style, color, pattern, texture, space, and lighting all contribute to the tone you want your home to convey. Last but not least is the fine art of *display*. This is the fun part, the part where you add the touches that instantly make your home unique: a favorite picture of a great-grandfather on an antique easel, a stained-glass window from the church where you were baptized, a family Bible rich with generational listings of family firsts. Display is all about making the most of your possessions.

Books are an essential feature in any living room. A great source of entertainment and interest, their varied sizes and colors also add warmth and character. I like to arrange books in rows interspersed with small stacks of five or six volumes. Place a vase or an antique plate on a stand next to the book stack. This looks more interesting and less like your local library.

An interesting display does not have to be expensive. Things like driftwood, stones, shells, and pine cones all have a decorative appeal when arranged imaginatively. Select a theme you love, and build a unique display around it. For example, I love the ocean, but my home in Dallas, Texas, is nowhere near an ocean. So for me, a large glass cylinder filled partially with ocean sand and unusual shells is a perfect reminder of time spent relaxing and listening to the waves. What whispers relaxation to you? Frame it, bottle it, and display it.

A collection of identically framed prints or drawings becomes a focal point when framed and mounted correctly. Sconces hung on either side of a mirror give a balanced look to any wall. Leaning pictures against a wall or table helps to offer a unique venue for your art.

Review the shelving in your home. Do you have what you need? Shelves are the backdrops for your treasures. Do you have enough of them, and are they lit properly? Shelves hung one foot below the ceiling around the perimeter of a room offer a great space for collections, books, and storage.

Pillows can also play a significant role in the decoration of a living room. The room's style will dictate whether they are piled high in a splash of color and pattern, or whether a more precise arrangement designed to coordinate with other fabrics is in order. Pillows can be easily made; in fact, just this week I found two place mats laden with beads at a store—at half price! Flipped inside out and sewn together, these place mats instantly became a pillowcase. For me, home décor boils down to always being on the lookout for great items at great prices, and thinking outside the ordinary.

Our ultimate goal is to create a space that gives us the best environment for offering hospitality to our family first and then to our friends. This is not about stuff! This is about feeling comfortable enough in your surroundings to be your best self, thus giving you the chance to share to your maximum ability.

SIMPLE SOLUTIONS

1. When setting the tone for your home, take time to decide what is truly important to you and your family. Study decorating magazines, books, Web sites, and television shows to jump-start this process.
2. Start a collection of books, candlesticks, photos of favorite places, porcelain boxes, china plates, or antique dolls. These make rich display items for your entry and living areas.
3. Use your hallway as an art museum to hang children's favorite artwork. You can find inexpensive frames at the dollar store.
4. Place votive candles in antique wine or champagne glasses.
5. Keep a chalkboard, chalk, and eraser at your back entrance for large reminders for your daily to-dos, messages to family members, and emergency phone numbers.
6. Stack a few old suitcases to make terrific side tables.
7. Place a few antique teacups down the middle of your dining table to make a perfect centerpiece.
8. When discovering your style and creating your home's tone, use all of your senses: taste, sight, touch, sound, and smell.
9. Place a long, smooth cedar board in the middle of your coffee table. Fill it with white candles of varied heights.
10. Keep clutter to a minimum so your eyes can rest.

CHAPTER SEVEN

The Kitchen Magician

I would cook dinner, but I can't find the can opener!

Home cooking. Aren't those two of the best words you've ever heard? That's what my family ate when I was growing up—home cooking, Southern style. My mother canned beets and green beans and made delicious pickles from the cucumbers in our garden. Her peach preserves melted in my mouth, and I loved to eat her apple butter right out of the jar.

Mom never put chips, deli meats, or pickles on the table in their containers. As a child, I thought she should just plop the entire bag of corn chips on the table, but she would say, "Our food looks so much better in bowls." Now I get it. Mom was using Martha Stewart ideas before they were chic!

That was then—and our "now" is a bit different. But I still want to create that atmosphere of warmth and good taste I experienced as a child. Can it be done in the fast lane? You bet. It just takes a little thought.

My experience as a food stylist taught me that with just a few key ingredients, you can catapult your kitchen hospitality from mediocre to magnificent. This chapter is full of my favorite recipes and tasty tips for making ordinary ingredients in your kitchen into something extraordinary! So when the doorbell rings, relax—you have this one in the pantry.

Let's take a look at some quick and tasty tips that might make Martha Stewart proud.

TOP TEN TORTILLA TIPS

The tortilla is your friend. I mean it! Keep some of those versatile, thin, round pancakes on hand, and you are good to go.

1. Tortilla Cups: Place six custard cups upside down on a cookie sheet. Spray the custard cups with cooking spray. Brush both sides of a six-inch flour tortilla with melted butter, place over each custard cup, and bake at 350 degrees for six to eight minutes or until browned. Cool. Fill the tortilla cup with scrambled eggs topped with bacon or chicken salad topped with crushed tortilla chips. You can also layer the tortilla cups with taco meat, rice, and lettuce, and then top with shredded cheese and tomatoes.

2. Tortilla Cookies: Cut a ten-inch flour tortilla with your favorite cookie cutters. Place the shapes on a cookie sheet that has been sprayed with cooking spray. Brush the tortillas with melted butter and sprinkle with cinnamon and sugar. These little cookies are your friends all year round. In January, fold the flour tortilla into fourths, take kitchen scissors, and cut triangles in sections around the perimeter of the tortilla. Open the folds, and you have a tortilla snowflake. In February, use heart-shaped cutters and red sugar. In March, shamrock shapes and green sugar. You get the idea!

3. Tortilla Club Sandwiches: Place a ten-inch spinach tortilla on a piece of waxed paper. Spread a thin layer of refried beans on the tortilla and sprinkle with cheese. Place a second tortilla on top and sprinkle with shredded chicken and chopped green onions; place another tortilla on top of the stack. Mix one tablespoon salsa with two tablespoons sour cream; spread over the tortilla. Sprinkle with a layer of shredded lettuce, crumbled bacon, and chopped tomato. Top with the last tortilla. Cut into wedges and serve.

4. Tortilla Lasagna: Place a layer of sun-dried tomato tortillas on the bottom of a glass 9 x 13 inch baking dish. Top with cooked ground turkey. Layer with flour tortillas and top with fresh or canned tomato sauce. Add a layer of ricotta cheese, green chilies, and cilantro. Add a layer of spinach tortillas. Continue alternating layers until your baking dish is full. Top with tomato sauce and shredded cheese. Bake at 350 degrees for thirty minutes.

5. Tortilla Dumplings: Place eight (eight-inch) corn tortillas on a cutting board and cut into half-inch strips. Chop a small onion and sauté it with garlic in two tablespoons of oil. Add three cups of chicken broth, one can of chopped green chilies, and two cans of chunk-style chicken. Add cumin and chili powder to taste, and bring to a boil. Cover, reduce heat, and simmer fifteen minutes. Add tortillas and one to two cups of Velveeta cheese. Simmer until the cheese melts. Serve.

6. Tortilla Crisps: Place several flavors of eight-inch tortillas on a cutting board, cut into fourths, spray with butter-flavored cooking spray, and top with shredded Parmesan cheese and sesame seeds. Cut in wedges and bake at 350 degrees for ten to twelve minutes or until crisp.

7. Tortilla Piecrust: Spray a nine-inch pie pan with cooking spray. Place four (eight-inch) tortillas in the pie plate, adjusting them evenly so that the tortillas come up onto the sides of the pie plate. Set your oven to 400 degrees and bake for five minutes. Remove the tortillas from the oven and layer with shredded chicken, corn, salsa, green chilies, crushed tortillas, and shredded cheese. Place in the oven for ten to fifteen minutes to warm through.

8. Tortilla Rolls: Spread an eight-inch tortilla with strawberry cream cheese, then sprinkle with chopped strawberries and mini chocolate chips. Roll tightly. Place on a cutting board and slice.

9. Fruited Nachos: Cut eight-inch tortillas into fourths. Brush each tortilla with melted butter and sprinkle heavily with cinnamon and sugar. Bake at 400 degrees until crisp. Make a fruit salsa by chopping a variety of your favorite fruit; add one teaspoon of chopped mint and a splash of your favorite fruit juice. Place a dollop of fruit salsa on top of each cinnamon crisp nacho. Top with sour cream or vanilla yogurt.

10. Tortilla Tarts: Place a ten-inch flour tortilla on a cutting board. Brush a thin layer of caramel sauce over the tortilla. Add thinly cut slices of apple, raisins, and crushed walnuts. Top with a tortilla. Brush with melted butter and sprinkle with a mixture of sugar, ginger, and nutmeg. Bake at 400 degrees for five minutes or until warmed through. Remove from the oven, cut into fourths, and serve with a caramel dipping sauce.

ANGEL FOOD CAKE—FIVE WAYS

Angel food cake is an American favorite. Tender yet sturdy, it's a perfect base for a variety of desserts. Most supermarkets carry angel food cakes in the deli or bakery, or you can make yours from scratch or with a mix. Here are five ways to take angel food cake beyond basic.

1. Peach Cake: In a large bowl, combine one 18.25-ounce package angel food cake mix with one 15-ounce can diced peaches and juice. (Do not add water.) Mix well. Pour into a nine-inch tube pan or two loaf pans. Bake according to directions on cake package. If desired, serve with whipped topping.

2. Fondue Kabobs: Cut a nine-inch angel food cake into two-inch cubes. Slide cubes onto a skewer, alternating cake with pieces of fruit. Serve with a melted-chocolate dipping sauce.

3. Angel Dainties: Place a long sheet of wax paper on the counter. Melt one cup milk chocolate in the microwave or double boiler. While the chocolate is melting, tear a nine-inch angel food cake into two-inch pieces. Pour one cup toffee bars into a shallow bowl. When chocolate is completely melted, dip each piece of angel food cake into the chocolate and then into the crushed toffee bars. Set on wax paper to dry. This also works nicely with melted white chocolate, chopped pistachios, and dried cherries.

4. Lemon Curd Rolls: Slice a nine-inch angel food cake into half-inch slices. Place each slice between two sheets of wax paper and roll until completely flattened. Spread

two teaspoons lemon curd over the surface of the cake and roll tightly. Serve with sorbet or with fresh raspberries.

5. Raspberry Angel Cheesecake: Tear a ten-inch angel food cake into small pieces and spread into the bottom of a 9 x 13 inch baking dish. Mix two cups confectioner's sugar, one 8-ounce package cream cheese (at room temperature), one teaspoon vanilla, and one cup milk until smooth. Fold in two cups whipped cream. Pour over cake pieces. Pour raspberries over all. Dust the tops of the berries with confectioner's sugar. Chill four hours or overnight.

FANCY DESSERTS THAT ONLY *LOOK* DIFFICULT

Maybe you're having the monthly book club meeting at your house or have been asked to supply a dessert for the PTA meeting. Don't feel like making the same old oatmeal cookies? Try these scrumptious desserts, sure to please even the picky palates.

FLOURLESS CHOCOLATE TORTE

7 ounces semisweet chocolate
1/2 cup fresh brewed coffee
8 ounces unsalted butter
1 cup sugar
4 eggs, beaten

Preheat oven to 350 degrees. Spray an 8-inch springform pan with cooking spray. Melt chocolate and coffee together over low heat. Stir in sugar. Cut butter into 6 to 8 pieces. Gradually stir into chocolate mixture. Remove pan from heat. Beat in eggs just until blended.

Pour mixture into the pan and bake for 35 to 40 minutes or just until set. The center of the cake may still be a little runny. Chill. Cake is easiest to cut when cold but should be served at room temperature.

FUDGY PUDDING SQUARES

3⅜ ounce chocolate pudding mix (cooked, not instant)
1 box chocolate cake mix
1 6-ounce bag semisweet chocolate chips
½ cup chopped pecans, optional

Prepare pudding mix according to package directions. Blend the dry chocolate cake mix into the pudding; stir to combine. Pour into a greased 9 x 13 inch baking dish; sprinkle with chocolate chips and nuts. Bake at 350 degrees for 30 to 35 minutes.

CHOCOLATE MOLTEN CAKES

20 dark chocolate miniature Dove bars, unwrapped
6 tablespoons butter
¼ cup sugar
2 eggs
¼ cup flour
2 cups vanilla ice cream, optional

Preheat oven to 400 degrees. Spray four (4-ounce) custard cups with cooking spray. Melt chocolate, butter, and sugar in top of double boiler over simmering water, just until melted. Add eggs and whisk until well combined. Add flour and mix well.

Distribute batter evenly among custard cups. Place cups on baking sheet. Bake for about 10 minutes. Sides should be set, but centers soft. Invert onto serving plates; serve with ice cream or whipped cream.

MINTED BROWNIES

1 box brownie mix
1 box Junior Mints
powdered sugar

Make brownies according to package directions. Line a mini muffin pan with baking papers. Fill the papers $\frac{2}{3}$ full. Place one Junior Mint into each uncooked brownie and bake according to package directions. Sprinkle with powdered sugar.

FAKIN' THE BAKIN'

Need some simple secrets for styling with store-bought items? The taste is sensational, but the time spent in preparation is minimal. The keys to success with these easy combos are simple: come up with your own designer name for your culinary treat, and always serve on an interesting plate or platter, preferably of heirloom quality.

ORANGE GINGER COOKIES

2 dozen store-bought gingersnap cookies
1 dozen orange-flavored Andes candies

Place one dozen gingersnaps flat side up on a cookie sheet. Open orange Andes candies and place on top of gingersnaps. Bake in a 350-degree oven long enough to slightly melt orange candies. Remove from oven and top with a second gingersnap cookie. Place these cookies in a container lined with colorful netting and give as a teacher gift.

FROZEN CHEESECAKE

1 frozen cheesecake—complete with wax paper sheets between each piece
1 cup chocolate morsels
2 tablespoons heavy cream
edible flowers (optional)

Place frozen cheesecake on a lovely china plate. Let it sit out enough to slightly thaw. Remove wax paper slice dividers. Gently, as if working with play dough, push the slices together. Using the back of a butter knife, rub out the slice marks on the top of the cake. (The goal is to make the cake appear as though it is not presliced.)

Place the chocolate in a glass measuring cup, add the heavy cream, and melt the chips and cream in a microwave. Stir to combine; keep stirring until the mixture is shiny. Pour over the cheesecake. If the slice marks are rubbed out really well, you will not need the edible flowers on the top of the cake. If your chocolate sauce falls into the crevices, garnish the top with flowers. Set this pretty cake in a hatbox, and it makes a great gift.

BABY CAKES

Wal-Mart's or Target's 6-inch prepared cakes
1 box Fruit by the Foot

Place the tasty baby cake on a gorgeous plate. Open one package of Fruit by the Foot. Unroll the candy. Place one section of the piece over the middle of the cake, stretching from one side of the plate to the other. Do the same thing across the other side (to resemble a package ribbon). Pinch off two-inch sections of the fruit by the foot. Fold in half and twist the bottom half together—this should resemble a loop. Keep making loops and place them in the center of the crisscrossed longer sections of candy (you are making a bow). A bow-topped cake makes a great buffet centerpiece.

DIXIE COOK'S TOP THIRTEEN "HAVEN HELPERS"

For a home that runs smoothly, we all need to remember that perfection is not the goal. We want a warm, welcoming environment in which we can focus on our friends and family. A little planning ahead can make this easier to do. Here are Dixie's top tips:

1. Food! Shop weekly and stock up. It's nice when there are always treats in the cookie jar and fresh fruit in the refrigerator. Stock your pantry with standard non-perishables to make quick dishes if needed. Keep a roll of refrigerated cookie dough on hand for special celebrations. Always have coffee, regular and decaf, and a variety of hot tea bags. Microwave popcorn makes a quick party!

2. Order—not necessarily cleanliness! Try to keep things in their places. Pick up and put away as you go so you don't have a major clean-up job at the end of the day. Do a five-minute decluttering of your main living areas before dinner. Empty the kitchen sink each night.

3. Light! Create a warm and inviting environment with lamps in nooks, dimmer

switches to control the atmosphere, welcoming porch lights at night, opened curtains in the morning, and candles whenever possible.

4. Books, newspapers, magazines! In all rooms!

5. Comfortable seating. Most people prefer comfort to the latest trend.

6. Clean sheets and fluffy pillows.

7. Devotion to guests or family members. Serve others. Take care of their physical needs; provide a listening ear and a hug when needed!

8. Smile! (This may take a meeting with God before family or company arrives.)

9. Conversation! Avoid discussing negative or difficult issues at the dinner table. Engage everyone in the conversation.

10. Good planning. When I had my first baby, my mom taught me that the first thing I needed to do each morning in the kitchen was to make all the baby's bottles for the day, then plan on what I would make for dinner that night. (Think I'll go make a Jell-O salad now.)

11. Put family before company. Often when having company, I get so busy with preparations for them, I neglect the kids' needs or I get snappy with my husband. My husband and kids are my most important ministry!

12. Prayer! Spend time with God, get rid of any sin, focus on Him, and let His love shine through you.

13. When I go visit friends, I like to take a small gift . . . and usually it is flowers from my yard. I bought two boxes of small Ball canning jars to use as vases—very inexpensive. I save ribbon and reuse it by tying it around the jar to make a bow. Zinnias make great cut flowers for these small jars; they are easy to grow, bloom all summer, and are so colorful. Many common shrubs have pretty branches, and when a variety of them are put together, they look pretty, even without flowers.[1]

SIMPLE SOLUTIONS

1. When planning meals, always include quick-fix options just in case you have more to accomplish than you have day (grilled cheese and canned vegetable soup with added fresh herbs for a homemade taste, scrambled eggs and grilled ham on toast, deli meats and cheeses served on warm canned biscuits).

2. Fresh herbs placed in a water-filled plastic cup will last longer in your refrigerator.

3. Freeze cans of your favorite fruits in heavy syrup—open both ends of the can and place frozen fruit in blender; purée for a good fruit ice dessert.

4. Keep refrigerated piecrusts on hand. A quick quiche is often the answer when you don't know what to make for dinner. It also is a great recycler of leftover chicken or turkey. With crumbled sausage or breakfast bacon mixed with eggs, milk, and cheese, this can be served for any meal.

5. Always keep chocolate chips in the pantry. They're good alone, or melted and poured over ice cream, or if you have time to bake cookies, you are ready with the chocolate.

6. Plastic resealable bags are a must for storing leftovers. Write the date on the bag, and you have easy storage with no cleanup.

CHAPTER EIGHT

Get Up and Grow!

Don't let artificial light and city streets keep you from noticing sunsets and sunrises, from experiencing the spring of new life and the harvest of fall. If you don't have a farm, at least have a window box or a few pots of earth.

—M. Basil Pennington, *A Place Apart*

Taking time to nurture a beautiful garden can be the ultimate source of relaxation. Here beauty and serenity coexist with fresh and fascinating foliage. A simple sanctuary can reflect your personality and your life, whether you're just starting to garden or have been maintaining your yard, window boxes, or containers for several years. Natural greenery creates an environment that is ripe for offering hospitality. Surrounding yourself with nature's beauty makes you feel good, and when you feel good, it's easy to offer that feeling to others.

Gardening offers us so much. It allows us to participate in a small part of God's creation. It gives us opportunities to share, teach, and give. But it also gives us a chance to reduce our fast pace, reflect, and enjoy a deeper harvest. Gardening teaches us to slow down a bit, to stop and smell the roses.

A plant that grows and takes shape is a bit like our lives when we are planted firmly in God. He tills, mulches, weeds, prunes, and repots us to reflect His image. Often He forces us to go at His pace. Just as we cannot rush the growth of a garden, we must wait on Him to guide and direct our growth. Part of this process depends on us. Just as one must go to the nursery to start the gardening process, we must go to God and ask His will.

Every branch that does bear fruit he prunes so that it will be even more fruitful.

—JOHN 15:2

For me, every season brings an enchanting trip to the plant nursery. I absolutely love walking into a greenhouse full of color, whatever the season. My favorite planting season is spring. After the drab winter months, it's exciting to mosey through plant after plant of new growth.

Being relatively new to the gardening scene, sometimes I have to visit the nursery several times to gather my ideas, color combinations, and the nerve to take on a new planting project. My first step is always the ferns. Once they're hanging on the porch, it feels like spring and inspires me for another planting adventure.

There are numerous types of gardens: cutting, ornamental, formal, kitchen, island, edible flower, entry, herb, country, and border. Each garden has endless possibilities, potential, and pleasure. What's your unique garden style?

CUTTING GARDEN

For many of us, a cutting garden would be the greatest luxury—having an abundance of flowers for indoor arrangements. One good way to accomplish this without compromising the look of your yard or porch is to establish a special garden just for cutting and bringing fresh flower fragrance and color inside. The main function of a cutting garden is production rather than landscape display. Choose plants that flower exuberantly and dependably. These are usually planted in rows for easy maintenance and harvest. The major flower in Texas is the annual, because it blooms for an entire season and the more you cut, the more it grows. When planting, choose a variety of colors, textures, and heights so your indoor bouquets will be interesting.

I hear you saying, "This is certainly not simple." You're right! So if a cutting garden is out of your realm of possibilities, you'll find inexpensive, long-lasting bouquets of flowers at grocery stores or warehouse clubs. (I've had bouquets last more than a month when the water was changed just once a week.)

For a brief stint in my college years, I lived in the home management house at Baylor University—a place where home economics majors had to live for six weeks and try out their skills at homemaking, cooking, gardening, and more. The house had a cutting garden specifically for creating arrangements in the home. Here I learned the joys of tending a beautiful garden and displaying fresh floral arrangements all the time. Shortly after that, I lived behind a historic home that had five acres of incredible gardens and six gardeners to care for the grounds. Fresh bouquets became a part of my everyday living, and I became determined to have a cutting garden when I owned my own home.

> *All that summer Miss Rumphius, her pockets full of seeds, wandered over fields and headlands, sowing lupines. She scattered seeds along the highways and down the country lanes. . . . The next Spring there were lupines everywhere. Fields and hillsides were covered with blue and purple and rose-colored flowers. . . .*
>
> *She had made the world more beautiful.*
>
> —BARBARA COONEY, *Miss Rumphius*

BEST CUTTING-GARDEN FLOWERS

- BABY'S-BREATH
- LARKSPUR
- LILY
- TULIP
- COSMOS
- SNAPDRAGON
- ZINNIA
- MARIGOLD

KITCHEN GARDEN

Kitchen gardens are food gardens located in a sunny spot, usually close to the kitchen door. This type of garden is generally a smaller-scale garden planted just for the purpose of immediate use on the stove. It's quite handy to duck out the back door and pinch a few fresh herbs for a salad dressing and a couple of flower stems for the tabletop. The petite size keeps this type of garden manageable yet ornamental. You can use perennial crops to provide multi-seasonal interest and structure to the garden.

No room for or interest in a kitchen garden? You can still keep some fresh herbs growing, like mint, chives, and basil. These can be grown in pots and placed on your window sill or your patio. Fresh mint finely chopped and folded into brownies, tossed into a fruit salad, or added to vinaigrette takes the ordinary up a notch or two. The same is true for chives: fold them into a store-bought quiche mixture or a thick stew, or use some to crust a salmon slice before grilling—delicious!

SALSA GARDEN

If you live in Texas for many years, you learn to love salsa or else you just don't dip your chips. Container gardens can do more than just be pretty; they can be fully functional for fresh ingredients. There are a few universal ingredients for salsa, and all can be grown on your deck, balcony, patio, or entry area. All you need are ceramic or plastic containers, potting soil, and plants.

JALAPEÑO PEPPERS
Jalapeño peppers are hot! They add a rich flavor that makes for a perfect salsa.
- Start seeds indoors five to seven weeks before the last average frost date in your area. Plant the seeds one-fourth inch deep, and keep them moist until the seeds germinate in two or three weeks.
- Transplant each pepper plant into an eight-inch pot at the same depth it was

growing in its original container. One plant will be sufficient unless you really like your salsa hot.

- Pick the peppers when they are two to three inches long.
- Wear plastic gloves when working with hot peppers; the juice from the peppers can create a burning sensation on the skin.

TOMATOES

Choose a tomato variety that yields fruit that is not too juicy. Tuscany, for example, yields abundant crops of plum tomatoes that have a deep red color and a rich flavor. The common sandwich tomato Better Boy is good as well.

- Start seeds indoors five to seven weeks before the last frost. Plant the seeds according to package directions.
- When the plants are five to ten inches tall, they are ready for transplanting.
- Use a twelve-inch pot so the plant will have plenty of room to grow. If the plant is a bit leggy, plant it deeper in the container to avoid roots forming along the stem.
- Place a tomato cage around the plant to keep it upright as it starts to grow.

TOMATILLOS

The tomatillo is the tomato's first cousin. It has a mild flavor and adds a crunchy texture to salsa due to its funny-looking husk around the outside skin. Tomatillos mature within seventy days and grow to about three feet tall.

- Start seeds indoors five to seven weeks before planting outdoors.
- Tomatillos are ready to harvest when the husks are beige or yellow.

CILANTRO

This herb is also known as coriander. Cilantro has delicate-looking leaves but a very strong, bold flavor that works nicely with salsa. People usually really like this flavor or don't like it at all.

- Grow cilantro from seeds in a container once you are ready to plant outside.
- Plant the seeds one-fourth to one-half inch deep, and keep the soil moist until they germinate in about seven to ten days.
- You can harvest cilantro while it is still quite small, usually within about six weeks.

ONIONS

Use a rectangular plastic container for a short row of onions. You can buy nursery-grown dry onion sets in bulk or in mesh bags.

- Bury the bulbs two inches apart. Press firmly into the soil.
- Harvest the onions when the tops fall over and dry.
- After harvesting the onions, lay them out in single layers to dry. Choose a shady spot to cure them. This allows them to develop a protective, papery wrapper.

Once your salsa garden is planted, find a sunny spot for the containers. Water everything well throughout the summer. Fresh salsa in little canning jars makes a perfect gift! Tie a little recipe around the jar lid using natural raffia.

GARDEN FRESH SALSA

Makes 3 cups

3 medium ears of corn, kernels cut from cobs, about 1¾ cups
½ cup onion, thinly sliced
1 large red pepper, diced
1 tomatillo, firm but ripe, diced
2 tablespoons canola oil
2 tablespoons fresh lime juice
2 tablespoons cilantro, minced
1 teaspoon white wine vinegar
1 teaspoon salt
¾ teaspoon cumin
¾ teaspoon sugar

Place all of the ingredients in a bowl and toss, taste, and adjust seasonings as needed. Refrigerate overnight for best flavor. Serve with chips or over grilled chicken, fish, or pork.

If the thought of making a salsa garden is out of the question for you, try this. Buy regular salsa and add fresh herbs like cilantro, chives, or mint. Ta-da! Homemade-tasting salsa. Add some sour cream, and you have a great dressing for a salad.

NINE STEPS TO PLANNING A PRETTY GARDEN

1. Plan your garden first. Is it the front yard you want to redo or spruce up? (No pun intended.) Is it the backyard? Is it both?

2. Read up on your region. The home-and-garden section of your local newspaper is a great source of information, as are magazines and the Internet. One mistake I made was choosing low-sun plants for the front yard, which received full sun most of the day. Knowledge of your region and your yard saves time, money, and extra work.

3. Choose plants that are low maintenance. Often, expensive nurseries have a great horticulturist who can answer questions. You might buy a few plants there and then fill in the rest from a cheaper source. Some home remodeling stores guarantee their plants for one year.

4. Keep in mind your budget and time restraints. You can spend a bundle rather fast. Make your plan and work it.

5. Try container gardening. This is a good way to add color in various areas, and you can always rearrange if you need color somewhere else. Try plants like snapdragons, zinnias, sunflowers, and impatiens.

6. Make sure you have the correct gardening tools. A good spade, shovel, rake, leaf rake, and hoe make the job simpler.

7. Don't forget to protect yourself as you beautify your yard. You will need gardening gloves, sunscreen, a lightweight hat, and lightweight clothes.

8. Water your plants, feed them, and watch for bugs. When unusual things begin happening with my plants, I pinch off a leaf and head to the plant doctor. They can usually look at a plant and decide what it needs to become healthy again.

9. Pull weeds regularly—everything looks better when a few weeds are pulled. It feels like a good haircut.

GETTING STARTED

Getting started can be intimidating when it comes to caring for plants. First of all, plants are not cheap, so you want to make sure you do all you can to keep them healthy. Second, you need a plan. Oftentimes nurseries will come out to your home and give you a landscape estimate, featuring the types of shrubs, flowers, and trees that would be best suited for your area. Hiring a nursery to landscape your yard is a great option if it is in your budget. If not, you can glean some interesting and creative ideas that you can implement yourself.

When creating your outdoor landscape, start by setting a budget. Then drive around your favorite neighborhoods and check out what other people have done. Look at the colors and shapes of their gardens. Look at the materials they used to create beds, borders, and lighting. Consider the sun exposure your plants will get. The area around a south-facing door will get harsh sun during the summer, and the heat will be intensified by nearby paving. Select plants that like the sun but do not need constant watering. Plant a small tree or two to offer some shade. Then consider your soil. If it is clay or sand, choose plants that thrive in that type of medium.

After you have made these assessments, you are ready to make the beds, place a decorative border, and begin planting.

GARDENING 101

- PLAN
- PREPARE
- PLANT
- CARE
- HARVEST

Go not abroad for happiness. For see it is a flower that blooms at any door.
—MINOT J. SAVAGE

GARDENING ACCESSORIES

The ornaments you choose for your garden offer the finishing touches to complete your outdoor surroundings. Gardening accessories add color, shape, texture, mood, and whimsy, all reflecting the interests and personality of the owners. They are also useful in establishing focal points and period style.

TRY THESE FINISHING TOUCHES FOR YOUR GARDEN:

- Animal motifs
- Informal art pieces
- Wildlife sculptures
- Gazing balls
- Birdbaths
- Benches
- Birdhouses
- Flamingos
- Statues
- Iron gates
- Hammock
- Ceramic plaques
- Wind chimes
- Watering cans
- Cherubs
- Recycled old wooden chair
- Unique planters

SIMPLE SOLUTIONS

1. Think of ways to soften walkways, steps, railings, and front doors.
2. Fill a brightly painted window box with pansies and ivy.
3. Place a large pot on your front stoop and fill with red and white geraniums.
4. Plant a climbing rose over your door; it offers relaxed grace and a good aroma.
5. Use strategically placed flowers to warn visitors about steps and landings.
6. Load various types of flowers and colors into one pot, making sure the plants all require the same care.
7. Always consider height when doing a container garden. Topiaries fly high, while ivy and ferns hang low.
8. Plant low-growing flowers around a stone walk. The color and foliage soften the edges of the rock and offer a colorful greeting.
9. Plant an edible landscape: vine tomatoes, runner beans, red and green lettuces, and containers full of herbs.
10. Hang baskets of flowers from the lamppost and on a sturdy branch of a large tree.

CHAPTER NINE

Designing an Inviting Entrance

Color is like food for the spirit—plus it's not addictive or fattening.

—Isaac Mizrahi

Let's pretend we are driving down your street. As we pull up to your home, what do you feel? Do you see a place where you want to come inside because the front yard, porch, and foyer whisper, *Welcome*? As the keeper of your castle, you have the opportunity to create an attractive entrance—one that makes you want to stop, get out, and relax. This, too, is hospitality: creating an environment from the inside out that invites people to stop and sit a spell.

Remember that funny show *The Munsters*? As the show opened, the family drove up to a horribly scary, overgrown, and dark front entrance. Now, that was the perfect recipe for keeping unwanted visitors at bay! In this chapter, we'll look at our homes' entrances—from the curb up.

ENTRANCE *EXTRAORDINAIRE*

The entry garden establishes the front yard as a welcome transition from the harried world to a place of tranquillity. It helps to set the tone of your home. This is where hospitality starts, by creating a welcoming environment. Try to design your entry garden to reflect the style or feel of your home. Use materials, such as brick or stone, to blend in with the surroundings. Choose plants that thrive best in the sunlight or shade this area receives. Lighting helps to make the garden show in the evening hours. It can also illuminate the path to your front door.

When planning your plants and flowers, remember that a good design is one that stays attractive and doesn't require much effort to maintain. An inviting entrance also enhances the value of your property. If your house has a formal style, choose a design featuring straight manicured paths, symmetrical plantings, ornate-looking benches, and elegant gates. Choose lots of greenery in your shrubs and small trees. If your home is not formal, let the landscape take on a more natural appeal. Curve the paths and driveway; build gates and fences that have a more rustic feel. Choose lots of colorful plants, and spread them around randomly. Be sure to think low maintenance! The right plant in the right spot copes well without constant care, pruning, and spraying.

Our first home was "landscape challenged." The boxwoods in the front beds were almost as big as our dining room—overgrown was an understatement! Looking at the bushes in the yard sort of reminded me of looking at the teeth of a big, smiling jack-o'-lantern. It took plenty of "vision" to see behind the nasty landscape design. While landscaping companies were available to help for a price that was out of our budget, Mark and I realized that with a few gardening shows under our belt and a trip to a great nursery, even *we* could make a mess look majestic.

CONTAINING YOURSELF

My front-porch entry garden consists of big terra-cotta pots filled with the flowers of the season. In spring and summer I use caladiums, variegated ivies, impatiens, asparagus fern, and geraniums. In fall and winter I use crotons, purple and white ornamental cabbages, and whatever other flower I find that is a unique color. When container gardening, remember that plants in containers dry out quickly, so place pots where you can conveniently water them as often as needed. Group the containers to save work and to create concentrated color. The entrance to your home is a perfect place for a container garden. The best news about a container garden is that it's movable. Need a pretty flower on the mantel? Grab it from your porch! Have a habit of rearranging items in your home? Your containers become a traveling splash of color.

WHY HAVE A FRONT-PORCH CONTAINER GARDEN?

- You can grow practically every type of plant in containers—from annuals and perennials to vegetables and herbs to trees and shrubs.
- Container gardening is so popular that nurseries now produce all kinds of potted gardens.
- It is easier to grow most of your culinary herbs in containers rather than the garden because you can walk out to the porch and snip what you need.
- Planting in containers helps you determine whether a given plant is one you might want to later plant permanently in your garden.

THE FRONT PORCH

The front porch offers a snapshot of those who live inside the house. Your porch can be a sign of a welcoming and open heart. Just glancing at the porch shows the personality of a home long before the door is opened. This is where your personal charm begins.

I've seen gorgeous wraparound porches complete with ceiling fans and rocking chairs stacked with overstuffed pillows. I've seen petite porches styled with beautiful flowering plants and cement stoops graced with brightly colored welcome mats. Whatever porch style you have, remember it's yours. This is where you welcome others into your life.

When I was growing up, our front porch had a big swing. I loved to take naps, read, and visit with friends on that swing. We had a table, chairs, and a teacart topped with a wicker lamp and a Boston fern. The dim light from the lamp cast a glow over the entire area, making it a desirable destination. To this day I fondly reflect on the warm, cozy feeling we shared in the comfort of our porch. It was a hospitable place. Not many people have porches like that anymore, but we can still create that feeling of warmth and friendliness.

PORCH PERK-UPS

- Purchase an inexpensive baker's rack and fill it full of colorful plants and pottery. Intersperse a few citronella candles to keep the bugs at bay.

- A wooden slatted swing or glider is a wonderful way to relax. Place one on the patio for a serene and relaxed touch. Fill it with fluffy pillows.
- Use brightly colored pillow cushions on your patio chairs, and change the pillows with the seasons. Buy them at a reduced price at the end of each season.
- Tender-sounding wind chimes make a lovely addition and a soft and beautiful sound on breezy days.
- For an old-fashioned welcoming touch, try painting your door bright red, glossy green, or shiny black.

DOOR DUTY

Does your front door look inviting? Whether with color, a fabulous wreath, a Christmas stocking, several ears of Indian corn, or an interesting light fixture—the front door has a big impact on visitors. How does yours look? The best test is to walk across your street and see if you like it. The next step is basic maintenance. Does your doorbell work? One of the cutest doorbells ever is at the home of my Bible fellowship teacher. When you ring the doorbell, it plays the Southern tune "Dixie." It just so happens that the lady of the house is named Dixie!

One thing to keep an eye out for is a dog paw or sticky finger smudge on your glass storm door. I often see that mess just as I open the door for guests. So if you have a glass storm door, hit it with a little Windex prior to your guests' arrival. Better yet, check it every few days.

FOYER MARCH

Once you are pleased with the outer portion of your entrance, consider your foyer or entry, if you have one. In our first home, the foyer was very small, but I had just enough room for an antique table against the wall. Above the table was a mirror in a gold-leaf frame with a large bow pretending to hold it up. This was a fun spot for me because I constantly traded out treasures to sit on the tabletop: tall pilgrims surrounded by baby pumpkins at Thanksgiving, a big painted rabbit holding a purple cabbage filled with colorful eggs for Easter, and a little Christmas tree filled with velvet bears for December. It was my personal display place.

In *Chris Madden's Guide to Personalizing Your Home*, Madden offers four basic principles that can guide you as you restyle or redesign your foyer.

1. Consider the *traffic*. Your foyer is a high-traffic area, so position furniture and other pieces carefully.

2. Keep the *maintenance* very simple.

3. Provide *storage* for coats, umbrellas, hats, and other outdoor gear.

4. Be *versatile*. Choose furniture that offers options, a place for glasses and keys, as well as ample space for a few of your favorite things.[1]

SIX WAYS TO CREATE A FABULOUS FOYER

1. Select a theme for your foyer. Some ideas are family pictures (for example, all in black-and-white with red mats), pet pictures, favorite scenery from your most cherished trips, or a year-by-year picture diary of your children. Uniquely framed and matted photos instantly add style to an entry.

2. Create an indoor garden mural down your hallway. Nail wooden pickets to the wall and stencil ivy and colorful flowers in between the pickets and above the pickets.

3. Put a chair rail down the middle of each wall on either side of the entry. Paint under the chair rail with one of your favorite colors.

4. Use the entryway for the children's art gallery. Frame their favorite art projects and hang them in the gallery.

5. Line the foyer with unique baskets. Place plants in some and magazines in others. Leave some baskets empty just in case you need a quick way to deliver a gift.

6. Display antique quilts. Affix quilts to the wall with special hangers or a quilt rack so as not to ruin the quilt.

SIMPLE SOLUTIONS

1. Place colorful pots on either side of your front door and fill them with an assortment of flowers: bronze, deep maroon, and golden mums, variegated ivy, paper-whites, geraniums, and asparagus fern.

2. Purchase a sturdy grapevine wreath for the front door. Recycle the wreath with just a change of silk flowers. Try matching the flowers on the wreath with the flowers in the pots beside the front door, or to the seasons.

3. If your front door has a window, drape the window with a beautiful piece of lace or a colorful silk scarf.

4. If your budget allows, purchase a gorgeous front door. Spotlight the door at night.

5. On the stairs leading up to your door, place graduated terra-cotta pots filled with brightly colored and fragrant flowers. Also include some rosemary or lavender—these herbs offer a fresh fragrance to your entry.

6. Place English ivy topiaries on either side of your front door to add definite grace. These can be used in any season.

7. Select a beautiful and colorful welcome mat that coordinates with your flowers.

8. If your front entry is petite, keep a flat basket of fresh herbs on your front door or a small basket of blooming plants next to the door. This softens the entrance without taking up much room.

9. Use an easel and chalkboard as a welcome sign. It can double as a message board, a menu board, and even a spot to place a holiday greeting.

10. Make pillows for a front porch bench using vintage dishtowels.

PART THREE

The Art of Sharing

CHAPTER TEN

Maximizing Ministry Moments

Hospitality is a sunbeam which may pass through a thousand bosoms without losing a particle of its original ray; nay when it strikes on a kindred heart, like the converged light on a mirror, it reflects itself with redoubled brightness. It is not perfected until it is shared.

—Jane Porter

As we've discussed, our hospitality ministry begins at home. It begins by nurturing the relationships that are closest to us, emotionally and spiritually. But when we walk out our door, our ministry expands quickly. Hospitality is sowing seeds of kindness toward others, no matter where you find them.

THE MINISTRY OF SHARING

Teaching children to share can be a chore. Sharing with others does not come naturally; it's a finely polished skill. We adults need to learn it too. What does it really mean to share? Mr. Webster defines *share* as "to partake of, use, experience, or enjoy with others."[1] So sharing with others involves experiencing part of life together.

So what does it mean to *minister*? The word sounds so churchy, but in reality ministry certainly is not limited to the confines of the church. My dictionary defines *minister* as "to give aid or service."[2] It is the service of the heart. Sharing and ministry together mean "enjoying others as an act of service," the very cornerstone of hospitality.

John Wesley was an incredible servant of God. His motto was "Do all the good you can, by all the means you can, in all the ways you can, in all the places you can, at all the times you can, to all the people you can, as long as you ever can." This is greatness. This is God's design.

In Rick Warren's book *The Purpose Driven Life*, he explains, "God is at work in the world, and he wants you to join him. This assignment is called your mission. God wants you to have both a ministry in the Body of Christ and a mission in the world. Your ministry is your service to believers and your mission is your service to unbelievers."[3]

For seven years Mark and I have belonged to a couples' prayer group. This group was started by R. J. and Edwina Patterson to help couples with young children grow spiritually and share each other's burdens. Once a month we meet in the Pattersons' home and partake of a delicious dinner Edwina has prepared. We relax, laugh, and eat. When dinner is finished, we move into their den and nestle into comfortable, overstuffed furniture with our notebooks and pens. One person begins sharing his or her needs for prayer, and we go around the room until everyone has listed their personal requests. We get on our knees and pray for our families, our country, our church, and our friends. The Pattersons share their spiritual maturity, their food, their home, and their lives.

The Pattersons' ministry is to believers, but Edwina's mission spreads worldwide. On her Web site, she shares the following story of how her simple hospitality has influenced many young men and women:

> Just a few short years ago, several young women came to me and asked me to begin mentoring them. They didn't feel equipped to meet the challenges that face families today: the fast pace of life that we have, the lack of morals in society, the complacency of failed marriages, the materialism, and the violence. They were looking for a role model, and I'm still amazed that they came to me for answers. But I guess they saw in me someone that was very approachable, nonthreatening . . . and a success story. My husband, R.J., and I have been married forty-two years. We have three grown children and seven grandchildren. These young women were watching the lives of our children and the way they were choosing to raise their own children, and they wanted to know what our secret was.
>
> What began as a ministry focusing on equipping/encouraging the Christ-centered home has evolved into so much more. It has developed into a ministry focusing on bringing men and women to the point of realizing that they need to redeem the time in their lives.

SEVEN WAYS TO REACH OUT TO YOUR NEIGHBORS

1. Borrow some sugar and return it twofold. Bring back a bag of sugar and a batch of freshly baked cookies or brownies.
2. Take an interest in your neighbors' lives and in the lives of their children.
3. Help coordinate an annual "dinner on the grounds." Ask the neighbor who has the biggest trees to host the outdoor event so there will be plenty of shade.
4. Invite your neighbors over for coffee and a snack. This simple gesture will give you an opportunity to get to know each other.
5. Have on hand a supply of ice cream, cookies, and lemonade, and invite the neighborhood children over to play.
6. Bake extra cookies during the holidays. Place them in Chinese takeout containers decorated with a bow, and deliver them to your neighbors.
7. If you are running to the store, phone a neighbor and see if you can pick up anything for them.

The ornament of the house is the friends who frequent it.

—Ralph Waldo Emerson

SIMPLE HOSPITALITY TO OVERNIGHT GUESTS

A great opportunity to maximize our ministry moments is when we are hosting overnight guests in our home. My friend Mindy Short has a fun and creative idea for practicing simple hospitality to overnight guests: she turns her home into a bed-and-breakfast! Here's how she does it:

> I wanted to set the tone of joy and fun from the moment my overnight guests entered the front door. With my creative juices flowing, I sat down at my computer and, lo and behold, The Way Down South B&B was open for business. My children's

rooms turned into suites. We had the Hawaiian Suite, the Sport Suite, the Cub Suite, the Bug Suite, and the Texas Suite. Door plaques were made via the computer, craft paper, and fun scissors.

When our guests arrived, they were greeted with a big "Howdy" and "Welcome to The Way Down South B&B. Please check your room assignment on the door, and I will direct you to your suite." Upon arriving at their room, they were all greeted with the rules and menu of the week. On top of each pillow was some chocolate candy.

This was the greeting on each door:

> Welcome y'all to The Way Down South B&B. Kick off yer boots and git comfy. Yer fixin' to have a good ol' Texas time enjoyin' one another's company. We're glad yer here and hope y'all enjoy yerself. Y'all will find all the comforts of home right at yer fingertips. Help yerself to anything you might need.

I informed them that each breakfast would be continental. Lunch would consist of a variety of sandwiches with all the fixin's. Then I proceeded to give out each day's dinner menu. This was less stress for me. . . .

My sister-in-law informed me that her family would like to put in their reservation for next year. This confirmed in my mind that their stay at The Way Down South B&B was a huge success! All it took was imagination, a computer, and the ability to set the tone of joyfulness and fun from the start. It's easy! Give it a try at your next gathering and watch the reservations pour in.[4]

MISSION KINDNESS

Have you ever been nourished by someone's thoughtfulness? Think for a minute. Write down what it was that meant so much to you. Can you think of someone who might need a small gesture of kindness from you?

Good intentions coupled with lack of action are a recipe for doing nothing. Creating a hospitality action plan is the key component of creating a ministry lifestyle. Here's how.

Get out your monthly calendar and schedule a day or a half-day for "mission kindness." Include your family and be flexible as to how you handle this process. Just the other day my mother was in the hospital and my young daughter had a high fever. It was one of those days when you feel as though you need to be two people. My sister-in-law called to say she was in the neighborhood and wanted to bring us two icy Slurpees. She came by, gave us the drinks, visited for a minute, and went about her day. It was a true mission of kindness, a day brightener. Did my sister-in-law plan this act of kindness months in advance? No. My sister-in-law has developed a lifestyle of sharing.

Think about what simple thing you could do today. Could you take a loaf of bread, a watermelon, or a magazine to a friend's home with a simple note stating, "I care for you. Thank you for the joy you add to my life"?

THINGS TO INCLUDE IN YOUR HOSPITALITY HANDBOOK

- NAME OF PERSON OR FAMILY
- IDEAS FOR HOSPITALITY
- PHONE NUMBERS FOR THE FOLLOWING:
  - *BAKERIES*
  - *GROCERY STORES*
  - *GIFT SHOPS*
  - *RESTAURANTS*
  - *CATERERS*
  - *FLORISTS*

SIMPLE SOLUTIONS

1. Create a plan to work sharing into your lifestyle. Make a sharing calendar, a month-by-month idea planner for reaching out to others.
2. Select a person or family who needs to see love and caring in action.

Show them love by sharing your food, books, videos, clothes, and most importantly, your time.

3. When preparing a meal, double your ingredients. Make two or three batches and freeze the extra portion for an emergency hospitality call.

4. Stock a gift closet for children and adults. This prevents being caught without a gift and saves money if you always buy when your favorite items go on sale.

5. Purchase numerous cards that fit every occasion. Mark your calendar with people's birthdays so when the time comes, you can grab a card and mail it.

6. Make a simple "thinking of you" phone call as a special pick-me-up to someone feeling down.

7. Pray for a friend regularly. Ask how you can pray for him or her specifically.

8. Purchase several inspirational books that are easy to mail. Mark a passage that has helped you through a difficult time, slip a note inside, and drop the book in the mail to someone who will be blessed by it.

9. Do something nice for a friend's children.

10. The key to maximizing ministry moments is being open to opportunities to extend kindness to someone else. In other words, pay attention!

CHAPTER ELEVEN

Entertaining in Style

Throwing a party is somewhat like having a baby—just because you made it through the last one alive is no guarantee now.

—Jean Kerr

A party is not a party without an appropriate atmosphere. Answering the door in sweats is not a great way to lead off a lovely evening! Neither should the host and hostess collapse with exhaustion following a special event with their friends and family. So what's the answer? Going out? Waiting until you receive the desired invitation? No! The answer lies with your attitude and a few simple suggestions.

RELAXED AND PEACEFUL ATMOSPHERE

A relaxed hostess sets the tone and overall atmosphere for the event. Does this come naturally when you're preparing a dinner party? Not likely. Strength from above is the only way to keep a calm spirit amid numerous hostessing responsibilities. On the day of the event, take a few moments in the morning to pray for your dinner party or special occasion. Pray for each guest who will be attending. Pray for peace in your own spirit, and watch this same peace spill over into your household.

Reflect on Philippians 4:6–7: "Be anxious for nothing, but in everything by prayer and supplication, with thanksgiving, let your requests be made known to God; and the peace of God, which surpasses all understanding, will guard your hearts and minds through Christ Jesus" (NKJV).

Remember, you don't have to strive for perfection as a hostess. You can be relaxed because when you move the focus off yourself, you can find incredible joy in entertaining others.

GRACIOUS GREETING

Although you may be busy in the kitchen, you have another job at the door. A gracious greeting is an important introduction to the evening. As hostess, you have several options. It's a good idea to plan your meal in such a way that when guests arrive, you are able to stand at the door and greet them. You can return to the kitchen once the guests have been properly welcomed to add the final touches to the food. There are times when the food preparation or the unforeseen keeps you in the kitchen; it is important at these times for your spouse or cohost to understand his or her responsibility at the door (and to stay there until the guests arrive).

The most important attire for the host and hostess is a lovely and sincere smile. Open the door with a smile, a handshake or hug, and warm words of greeting such as, "We are so glad you could join us this evening." You may want a designated area for coats and purses in order to easily assist your guests with their belongings. Offer beverages (and hors d'oeuvres, if you like), and introduce guests to each other. Telling a little background about the guest is a great way to get a conversation off to a good start. If you still have work to do in the kitchen, present the beverages and hors d'oeuvres in the kitchen in order for you to chat and work while your guests enjoy their goodies.

SIMPLE SCHEDULE OF EVENTS

As hostess, it is wise to plan a simple schedule for the evening. Your guests will feel at ease knowing that you have the evening planned and in place. It's rather disconcerting to attend a dinner party where the hostess asks her guests, "Do you think we should eat now?" or, "I wonder where everyone should sit?" These are plans that should be made before your guests arrive. If the party includes an activity or game or gift opening, then the "where" and "when" of these agenda items should also be preplanned. Remember to stay flexible if everything doesn't go as you thought it would!

Another helpful schedule to create is one for the day of your dinner party. This schedule is for you only. On this agenda, you map out the timing of when you need to make certain dishes, when to set the table, and how much time you need for baking, so the dishes are finished at the same time. Most importantly, don't forget to spend some quiet time with the Lord, praising, thanking, and lifting each one of your guests to Him. A bubble bath could be another wonderful treat to work into your day.

TABLE APPOINTMENTS AND FOOD SERVICE

After establishing a calm spirit for entertaining, it is time to decide the most comfortable way for you to appoint your table and serve your guests. The traditional place setting is arranged as follows: forks to the left, beginning at the outside edge according to the order in which they are to be used. Knives go on the right and are always placed directly beside the plate with the blade turned toward the plate. Spoons are placed to the right of the knife, beginning at the outside edge in order of use. If the table looks too crowded, try putting the dessert fork and spoon at the top of the plate as the English do. Water and iced tea glasses go above the knife and spoons, at the upper right-hand corner of each plate. Napkins are traditionally placed to the left of the forks, or you may want to be creative and place the napkin in the glass, hang it on the chair, or stand it on the plate.

The old rule for serving is to take away from the right of the guest and place or pass on his left. However, graciousness is our goal, so if you cannot easily serve this way, remember that you're not trying to be perfect! No one is grading your performance. It's your dinner and your table, so do what works best and is most convenient for you.

If you are inviting more than eight guests to be seated at the main table, you may want to consider buffet service. Your buffet can be served on a sideboard or in the kitchen. You decide where you feel comfortable, how your food will stay the warmest, and how your entertaining area will best accommodate your guests. Add a few decorations to your buffet table to accent the theme of your meal, and you are

off to a marvelous and memorable serving start. For younger kids, you may want to prepare their plates in advance, while older children can serve themselves from a special kids-only buffet or the adult line.

TABLE CONVERSATION

As mentioned earlier, your guests' enjoyment and comfort are the most important ingredients to a successful party. Lively conversation and shared interests make for a wonderful evening. Remember, you are not on your own here; these are the people for whom you have prayed earlier, so rest in the fact that God is present and presiding over His children.

If your guests are not acquainted with one another, you can highlight various happenings in each guest's life that would be appropriate for dinner conversation. Perhaps guests could share how they know the host couple, how many children they have, or what interesting trips they have experienced. The host and hostess need to discuss these topics prior to the evening so they can share the responsibility of facilitating memorable dinner conversation.

Place cards are a welcome way to help your guests find their intended seat without confusion. Although they are not necessary, place cards help you as a hostess to seat your guests in a way that will encourage good conversation. Gregarious people placed strategically among shy ones can keep the table flowing with frivolity. You may also use your place cards to inscribe a conversation booster question on the back. Ask your guests to read their question and give the answer to those sitting nearby.

If you desire your event to be an adult evening of conversation, set up a kids' table in a different room to keep interruptions to a minimum. Consider hiring a baby-sitter to help with younger ones. A teenager from the neighborhood can keep the children in control during the party—and you might even have her arrive early to help while you're getting ready for the evening.

GRACIOUS GOOD-BYES

Your graciousness upon the completion of your entertaining becomes the beautiful ribbon on the box of a great evening. Show deep appreciation for the good visit with your guests, help gather their belongings, and walk them to the door. As with the warmth of a genuine greeting, the sincerity of a gracious good-bye helps to solidify a good evening from beginning to end. Simple words such as, "It was a delight to have you with us tonight" or, "What a blessing to have you in our home" provide a positive conclusion to a harmonious event.

BEYOND HARRIED HOSPITALITY

- RELAXED AND PEACEFUL ATMOSPHERE
- GRACIOUS GREETING
- SIMPLE SCHEDULE OF EVENTS
- TABLE APPOINTMENTS AND FOOD SERVICE
- TABLE CONVERSATION
- GRACIOUS GOOD-BYES

UPTOWN HOSPITALITY

Several years ago I was invited to a lovely home for a Sunday brunch. The home was enormous; every decorating detail had been attended to. This hostess was gifted not just in decorating or food preparation but in the art of people.

As each guest arrived, the hostess graciously acknowledged and introduced the guests to one another. She then invited everyone to the long and well-appointed dining room table. As each guest was seated, she explained how her family knew him or her and one special thing about the guest's life. She made a declaration: "The food is on the buffet; please help yourself, but that is secondary. We want to visit and get to know each other and enjoy the fellowship we have as believers." Suddenly, the large yet exquisite dining room became smaller as the hostess's gentle spirit put each guest at ease. I had experienced real-life hospitality.

Whatever is lovely . . . think about such things.

—PHILIPPIANS 4:8

DOWN-HOME HOSPITALITY

Hospitality doesn't have to be fancy. My mother, Sarah Cabaniss, shares a story that adds a different dimension to hospitality in action:

> Many years ago, I traveled as an associate for the North Carolina Baptist State Convention. I was privileged to be invited to lovely and prestigious homes in many different states. The churches seemed to seek out the church leaders most capable of royally entertaining, and I loved it! The most memorable visit was in a very tiny town in the mountains of North Carolina. The home was small and unimpressive. As we knocked on the door, a smiling middle-aged lady wearing an apron opened the door and, my—the warmth and love we felt! As the lady took off her apron, she announced that everything was ready and began pulling chairs to the table . . . rocking chairs. She arranged the rocking chairs around the table and began serving the food. Country ham and homemade biscuits were in abundance along with vegetables and desserts. I still remember how the tiredness of travel, conferences, and concerns of the day melted away as we ate, laughed, and exchanged delightful stories. We were one in fellowship.

> *Silver or gold I do not have, but what I have I give you.*
>
> —ACTS 3:6

MANLY HOSPITALITY

Often in our culture, we are accustomed to women being responsible for the fine art of hospitality. Cookbooks, HGTV, Web sites, and magazines are geared mostly to women—especially married women. Please consider that the heart of a servant is just as apt to be found in a man as in a woman. Single or married men can be encouraged to become involved in hospitality too.

In fact, when my husband and I were dating, he invited me to his apartment for a gourmet dinner. I was quite impressed just at the thought of him cooking. I was traveling around the South doing cooking shows when we began dating, so you could say food was a real interest. Mark knew this and always arranged incredible dates at fancy restaurants. One thing we had in common was that we both loved to share delightful meals in lovely surroundings. Needless to say, my interest was piqued when given the opportunity to review Mark's kitchen talents. When I arrived, delicious smells filled the air. Pots, pans, and tea towels filled the kitchen. The dining table looked elegant with candles and borrowed china. We began our meal with a creamy lobster soup and continued with a pastry-wrapped beef tenderloin. The grand finale was amaretto chocolate cheesecake with fresh raspberries. I was quite pleased and somewhat amazed. This guy really understood hospitality and fine dining—what a catch!

As I began to compliment his efforts, Mark began to laugh hysterically. He took my hand, walked me into the kitchen, opened the refrigerator, and showed me numerous takeout containers. He had purchased the whole shebang and dirtied the pots and pans while pretending he had had a long day in the kitchen. So, you see, hospitality can be shared whether the food is prepared in your kitchen or purchased as takeout—fancy or not. It's all about sharing your heart, your home, and a good dose of humor.

Share your life, and find the finest joy man can know. Do not be stingy with your heart. Get out of your self into the lives of others, and new life will flow into you—share and share alike.

—JOSEPH FORT NEWTON

SPORTS-FAN HOSPITALITY

For the rest of this chapter, I'd like to walk you step-by-step through one of my favorite types of gatherings: a tailgate party! I've included a menu, recipes, shopping lists, detailed instructions, and a schedule. This particular event can be adapted to host at home, and you can certainly be creative in planning your own menu. I'm including this as an example of how to plan and prepare for a fun event with your guests.

Fired-up football fans flock to stadium parking lots in loaded-down sports utility vehicles weekend after weekend with their families in tow. Camaraderie of old friends and classmates is one goal of the age-old tradition of tailgating; achieving alfresco ambiance on the asphalt is another.

Plan a fun and festive theme to create the mood and to help set the pace for the entire tailgating experience. As with any outdoor entertaining, use the unexpected to add spice to the meal. A note: the following menu might seem a bit fancy for a tailgate party! I'm including it so you can see that simplicity can be achieved with thoughtful planning—it doesn't mean you have to settle for mediocre food.

Menu:

Pecan-Crusted Chicken with Blackberry Ketchup
Corn and Black Bean Confetti
Three-Potato Salad with Bacon
Sesame-Cheese Breadsticks
Spicy Brown Sugar Angel Food Cake with Cinnamon Cream
Flavored Waters with Fresh Orange Slices

Kids' Menu:

Fried Chicken Pitas
Corn Cups
Potato Pancakes
Cheesy Breadsticks
Angel Dainties

Market List:

Staples
Flour
Cake flour
Powdered sugar
Brown sugar
Sugar
Pecans
Breadcrumbs

Spices
Salt and pepper

Thyme
Cloves
Ginger
Cayenne pepper
Dry mustard
Cream of tartar
Pumpkin pie spice
Vanilla
Cinnamon
Sesame seeds

Fresh Produce
Mushrooms
Green onion
Red pepper
Cilantro
Oranges
Golden potatoes
New potatoes
Sweet potato
Red apple
Celery

Dairy
Butter
Whipping cream
2 dozen eggs
Cream cheese
Parmesan cheese

Frozen Foods
Corn
Blackberries

Meat
3 pounds chicken breast
  fillets
1 pound chicken breast for
  kids' pitas
Bacon

Condiments
Apple vinegar
Mayonnaise
Mustard

Canned Goods
Black beans

Drinks
Flavored waters

Breads
Pita bread

Prepared Foods
Prepared angel food cake

COUNTDOWN TO KICKOFF

Four days ahead:
Gather all serving and decorating materials.
Purchase or borrow an ice chest.
Make a checklist for all foods and items to pack.
Make sure you have supplies for the kids' activity.

Three days ahead:
Purchase groceries.
Prepare blackberry ketchup, store in airtight container, and refrigerate.
Prepare cinnamon cream, store in airtight container, and refrigerate.

Two days ahead:
Prepare the Spicy Brown Sugar Angel Food Cake; store in airtight container.
Prepare bacon for the Three-Potato Salad; cool, wrap tightly, and refrigerate.
Prepare Angel Dainties for the kids; store in airtight container.
Prepare Sesame-Cheese Breadsticks (leave off the sesame seeds for the kids);
    store in airtight container.

One day ahead:
Prepare the Three-Potato Salad and Potato Pancakes for the kids.

Prepare the Corn and Black Bean Confetti and Corn Cups for the kids.
Prepare the Pecan-Crusted Chicken; place on baking pan and bake.

Morning of:
Prepare Fried Chicken Pitas.
Fill ice chest with ice.
Ice down the drinks.
Slice the oranges; wrap tightly.
Follow your checklist for packing the pre-prepared dinner.

PECAN-CRUSTED CHICKEN

3 pounds chicken breast fillets
1/4 teaspoon salt
1/4 teaspoon pepper
3 teaspoons butter
1/4 cup mushrooms, chopped
1/4 cup green onion, chopped
1/4 cup cream cheese
1 teaspoon mustard
1 teaspoon fresh thyme
1 cup pecans, chopped
1/2 cup breadcrumbs
3 tablespoons butter, melted

On a hard surface, pound chicken; sprinkle with salt and pepper; set aside. In a small skillet, melt butter. Add mushrooms and onion; sauté until tender. Cool. Mix cream cheese, mustard, and thyme. Spread on the pieces of chicken and fold each fillet over, pressing the edges to seal. Mix pecans, breadcrumbs, and parsley. Dip chicken into remaining butter; roll each piece in pecan mixture to coat evenly. Bake in a greased baking dish at 375 degrees for 35 minutes.

BLACKBERRY KETCHUP

¾ cup frozen blackberries

3 tablespoons apple vinegar

3 tablespoons brown sugar

¼ teaspoon ground cloves

¼ teaspoon ground ginger

⅛ teaspoon cayenne pepper

¼ teaspoon salt

2 teaspoons butter

Mix berries, vinegar, and water in a saucepan and bring the mixture to a boil. Lower temperature and simmer for 10 minutes. Sieve out the seeds, rub out berry pulp, and return the mixture to saucepan. Mix remaining ingredients, and simmer 30 minutes until thicker. Pour into jar and seal. Refrigerate.

CORN AND BLACK BEAN CONFETTI

(Serves 4)

¼ teaspoon ground ginger

¼ teaspoon dry mustard

¼ cup sugar

⅓ cup vinegar

1½ cups water

1 15-ounce bag frozen corn

1 15-ounce can black beans

2 tablespoons minced green onion

2 tablespoons red pepper, chopped

1 tablespoon cilantro, chopped

Combine ginger, mustard, sugar, vinegar, and water in medium bowl; stir until thoroughly blended. Add corn, black beans, onion, red pepper, and cilantro, stirring to combine. Cover and refrigerate until chilled.

THREE-POTATO SALAD WITH BACON

(Serves 6 to 8)

3 golden potatoes

6 new potatoes

1 medium sweet potato

$\frac{1}{2}$ cup celery, thinly sliced

1 large red-skinned apple, cored and diced

$\frac{1}{2}$ cup mayonnaise

1 teaspoon mustard

$\frac{1}{2}$ teaspoon orange peel, grated

2 tablespoons crisply cooked bacon, crumbled

Place potatoes in a 3- to 4-quart pan. Cover with water and bring to a boil over high heat. Cover, reduce heat, and cook until tender—about 20 minutes. Check potatoes often, because some will cook faster than others and may need to be removed. Drain.

When potatoes are cool, peel and cut them into $\frac{1}{2}$-inch cubes. In a bowl, combine potatoes, celery, and apple. In a small bowl, stir together mayonnaise, mustard, orange peel, and bacon. Pour mayo mixture over potatoes; stir to combine. Cover and refrigerate overnight.

SPICY BROWN SUGAR ANGEL FOOD CAKE WITH CINNAMON CREAM

(Serves 12)

13 egg whites

$1\frac{1}{2}$ teaspoons cream of tartar

$\frac{1}{4}$ teaspoon salt

$1\frac{1}{2}$ cups brown sugar

$1\frac{1}{2}$ teaspoons vanilla

1 cup cake flour, sifted

2 teaspoons pumpkin pie spice

Place egg whites in a mixing bowl and begin beating, gradually adding cream of tartar and salt. Beat until soft peaks form. Add brown sugar and vanilla. Beat well. Sprinkle flour over egg white mixture $1/3$ cup at a time, beating well after each addition. Add pumpkin pie spice. Pour batter into a 10-inch tube pan and bake at 375 degrees for 30 to 35 minutes, or until cake springs back from your touch. Invert pan and cool for 40 minutes. Loosen cake from sides of pan using a narrow metal spatula. Drizzle cake with cinnamon cream.

CINNAMON CREAM

2 cups whipping cream, whipped
2 tablespoons powdered sugar
$1\frac{1}{2}$ teaspoons cinnamon

Mix cream and sugar together. Slather on cake. Sprinkle with cinnamon.

SESAME-CHEESE BREADSTICKS

(Serves 12)
$3/4$ cup butter or margarine, softened
2 cups all-purpose flour
1 teaspoon salt
2 dashes cayenne pepper
ice water
1 cup sesame seeds
$1/2$ cup grated Parmesan cheese

Cut butter into flour mixed with salt and cayenne pepper. Sprinkle ice water over dough and toss with a fork until dough holds together. Roll out dough on a floured board to $1/8$ inch thickness and cut into strips. Place on an ungreased cookie sheet; sprinkle generously with sesame seeds. Bake at 325 degrees for about 15 minutes. Begin removing from pan; while still hot, sprinkle with cheese.

INVITATIONS

Build the excitement for a sensational sports event by making football-shaped invitations, with one side giving the party information and the other side listing the top ten reasons your football team will defeat their opponent. You can make this idea fit any sport using the appropriate ball or equipment.

AMBIANCE ON THE ASPHALT

Cover the trunk of your vehicle or card table with a tablecloth or blanket sporting your favorite team's colors. Add coordinating plates, utensils, and cups to match the theme colors. Balls, pompoms, streamers, and pennants will add to the décor as you open up the back door of your vehicle. You can find fun sports paraphernalia at your local party store. Plastic bowls in the shape of footballs and napkins with footballs or even team emblems will carry out the theme. Keep it simple and festive.

KIDS' KORNER

Two, four, six, eight—even the kids can tailgate! The kids will have loads of fun as they help you prepare for this memorable event. This easy-to-do craft will keep the future star athletes occupied while you prepare your all-star menu.

MAGNIFICENT MEGAPHONES (AGES 2–5)

You will need:
Colored poster board
(preferably team colors, one per every two children)
Stickers
Markers
Tape (optional)

Before the game, cut sheets of poster board in half. Roll up each half-sheet of poster board into a cone shape and tape together. Allow the little ones to decorate their megaphones using stickers and markers on a covered table near your work area. Let each child make several megaphones, one for each guest. Kids and adults alike will take great delight in cheering through their new megaphones!

A CLOSING THOUGHT

As you plan this fan-filled event, you might like to know that Scripture tells us we are all participants in a sport—the race of life. The writer to the Hebrews urged, "Therefore, since we have so great a cloud of witnesses surrounding us, let us also lay aside every encumbrance, and the sin which so easily entangles us, and let us run with endurance the race that is set before us, fixing our eyes on Jesus, the author and perfecter of faith, who for the joy set before Him endured the cross, despising the shame, and has sat down at the right hand of the throne of God" (Hebrews 12:1–2 NASB).

SIMPLE SOLUTIONS

1. When entertaining unexpected guests, hit the highlights: clean bathroom, lit candles, contained pets, dimmed lights, and designated no-go zones.
2. Eggs are the fastest things to cook; add cream cheese and chives to make them fancy (3 eggs, 1 tablespoon cream cheese, 1 teaspoon fresh snipped chives).
3. Keep serving plates warm by placing them on the dry cycle in your dishwasher.
4. Using a paint pen, write the name of your dinner guests on a small, clear bud vase and place a single flower in each vase in front of the plate. This will double as place card and centerpiece for your table.
5. Melt your favorite jelly and use it to baste meat.
6. Soften butter and mix in chopped mint, cranberries, and minced walnuts; form the softened butter into a ball and serve with hot rolls.

7. Freeze mint leaves in ice trays and serve with your favorite flavored tea.

8. Keep a rainbow of colored plastic wraps on hand to add color to your covered foods.

CHAPTER TWELVE

Kid Connection

As parents set the example, children can mature into happy hosts and hostesses who enjoy practicing simple hospitality.

It's important to teach children about hospitality from a very young age. One of the greatest ministries for teaching children the heart of hospitality is the "shoebox" ministry of Samaritan's Purse. This ministry has become a tradition with our family. Operation Christmas Child brings joy and hope to children in desperate situations around the world through gift-filled shoeboxes and the good news of God's love. Samaritan's Purse provides an opportunity for people of all ages to be involved in a simple, hands-on missions project while focusing on the true meaning of Christmas: Jesus Christ, God's greatest gift. Along with shoebox gifts, millions of children are given gospel booklets in their own language. In 2003, more than 6.6 million shoebox gifts worldwide were collected and distributed to children in some ninety-five countries.

Bob Pierce began the ministry of Samaritan's Purse in 1970. The mission statement penned in his Bible while returning from visiting suffering children in Korea read: "to meet emergency needs in crisis areas through existing evangelical mission agencies and national churches." What is so interesting to me is that this ministry is using children to reach children in countries they cannot even find in a world atlas. A prime example of hospitality to go![1]

GIVING TEACHES

....

- A SERVANT'S HEART,
- GENEROSITY,
- SHARING,
- KINDNESS, AND
- RESPECT FOR OTHERS.

So many valuable lessons can be learned when we reach out to help others! Teaching values can be fun, with just the right activities.

SERVING OTHERS

Everyone in our world has needs. God created us to help each other. Some have physical needs such as food, clothing, or housing. Others may need someone to talk to when they are lonely or a hug from someone when they are sad. There are so many ways of helping others. Here are a few party ideas to help you reach out and serve.

FOOD BANK PARTY

Helping people during the holidays is great, but there are agencies that help people all through the year, such as your local food bank.

Before you have your party, look in your telephone directory to find a food bank near you. Many of them are listed under community service organizations or helpful numbers. Call a local food bank to find out what types of food donations they need and where and when you can deliver them.

Invite several friends over to do a fun cooking activity and to donate food to a local food bank. Ask each person to bring two or three items to donate to the food bank. Peanut butter, canned soups, canned meats, and canned vegetables are good choices.

After collecting the food for the food bank, make some cookies from prepared cookie dough. (Remember, sugar-cookie dough is perfect for mixing in your favorite candies.) Wrap half the cookies in colored plastic wrap, and take them to give as a special treat to the people who work at the food bank. Return to the party and enjoy the remaining cookies.

TEACHABLE MOMENT

As each child arrives with his or her donation, thank the child for feeding the people who are hungry. Put the food into a big basket or box with a bow on it. Explain that the food will go to people who don't have enough to eat, people who might otherwise go hungry.

NURSING HOME PARTY

People living in nursing homes delight at seeing young, smiling faces. A servant's heart is a welcome sight to an older person. A smile is encouraging, and a child's enthusiasm for life can lift spirits. Don't underestimate the value of visiting a nursing home!

Contact the social services director or activities director at a local nursing home. Find out about special needs the residents may have and plan a good time for a visit.

Invite a few friends to visit the nursing home with you. Before you go, make pretty greeting cards to give to the residents. Afterward, go to an ice-cream shop and talk about whom you met and how your conversations went.

TEACHABLE MOMENT

Consider starting an adopt-a-nursing-home program in your school, church, or neighborhood. The nursing home residents will not be the only ones to benefit from this experience. Talk to the social services director about giving residents opportunities to make small gifts for the kids.

KID-TO-KID HOSPITALITY

Since I have an only child, I consider it extremely important for my daughter to learn proper interaction with other kids. Entertaining friends at home has helped her learn valuable life skills like planning and taking a backseat to guests' preferences. For example, if our daughter wants to watch a video but her friend prefers playing outside, we remind her to graciously accommodate her guest as much as possible. (*Graciously* is the key word.) When planning a visit, we go through a verbal checklist:

- Bedroom picked up?
- Home care done?
- Homework completed?
- Snacks and meals planned?
- Entertainment ready? (inside or out)
- Ministry opportunities or needs considered?

Our goal in making guests comfortable is to mirror Jesus's love so they will desire to know Him better. Parents also play a key role when young guests arrive. As Proverbs 17:1 reminds us, "Better a dry crust with peace and quiet than a house full of feasting, with strife." Parents need to be on their best behavior too—no bickering, complaining, or grumbling about household hang-ups. Instead, we should smile, be friendly, and create a warm and welcoming environment.

ENTERTAINING WITH KIDS

Hospitality with children can be boiled down to one word: *manners*. For adult gatherings, teach your children to let adults initiate conversations and to serve guests first helpings. When children have reached the preteen age, ask for their input in planning adult visits. Their opinions and assistance make things run more smoothly. If you're running late or feeling frazzled, your preteen or teenage children are often more creative in areas like these: meal menus, background music, games or entertainment, home decorating, and furniture arranging.

Working together to make our home a haven for guests cements the spiritual and emotional bonds shared by the family. Sometimes my family prays before a visit from friends with certain needs, as instructed in Proverbs 16:3: "Commit to the LORD whatever you do, and your plans will succeed."

Kids can help out in many ways when visitors are expected:

- Greet guests.
- Hang up coats.
- Offer beverages or snacks.
- Usher younger children to a play area and watch them.
- Provide teens access to video games or television.
- Assist elderly guests with steps or bundles.

Teaching children to be responsive to others and to trust each event to God's control helps them become proactive in dealing with issues in the privacy of their home before encountering them unexpectedly in the world beyond our door.

To entertain children so you can visit with adults, have some of these:
- Computer games
- Building toys or kits
- Swimming or basketball
- Videos or DVDs
- Books or magazines
- Imagination, dress-up, or made-up games

ADULT-TO-CHILD INTERACTION

When adult guests interact with our kids, we expect our young ones to show interest or appreciation. Children should come to say hello and good-bye to guests, and they should send thank-you notes for gifts. When my family receives thank-you notes that mention our daughter by name, I point out to her the value of her contribution to the hospitality.

Some adults arrange for their kids to eat earlier or separately, which is a great idea sometimes. Since my husband and I want our daughter to glean the benefit of adult interaction and develop social and communication skills, we often include the children when we entertain. With training and oversight, children can mature into cheerful hosts who win smiles and make others feel welcome.

SEVEN WAYS TO HAVE A SUCCESSFUL PARTY WITH KIDS

1. Include them in the planning.
2. Give them age-appropriate jobs.
3. Peruse Web sites for fun ideas.
4. Have all supplies on hand for your chosen activities.
5. Appoint an adult or teenager to be the activity helper.
6. Review your party manners prior to guests' arrival.
7. Have clothes selected and ready.

FOLLOWING JESUS'S EXAMPLE

Hospitality puts children into a line of spiritual development that helps them honor God and follow Jesus's example—particularly when we remember one of His final earthly meetings with the disciples when Jesus cooked breakfast for them on the shore as they fished. It was during that special time that He gave them the Great Commission and erected the pillars of the Christian church. While our visits may seem less important by contrast, we will still do well to follow Christ's example and teach children to respect guests. Hospitality is not only a virtue; it's a necessity.

Joining a ministry to teach miraculous giving, creating a servant's heart, and practicing good manners are all components of the package for practicing hospitality. Gifts to children also show affection and kindness. Here are some suggestions when a child needs a little special something from you.

REACHING OUT TO KIDS

There are so many occasions on which we can show kids we care. Sometimes these are important "special days" such as a birthday. Other times, we need to reach out in support during difficult times. Here are some ideas for sharing hospitality with children and celebrating your friendship with them.

JUST BECAUSE YOU'RE MY FRIEND

An edible alphabet is cute, quick, and fun. A child loves to hear and see his or her name, and making it edible adds imagination as well as education. Purchase a prepared pound cake and slice the pieces about one-inch thick. Cut the child's name out of the slices with alphabet cookie cutters (available at craft stores). Sprinkle with colored powdered sugar and place in a tie box.

CHILDREN GOING TO SCHOOL

For the kindergarten kid, purchase a monogrammed backpack and fill it with a writing tablet, fat pencils, and a simple, nonperishable snack. If the young person is heading off to college, wrap a couple of tickets to the movies or a sporting event in a box of stationery that is filled with college stickers and stamps.

Nothing works better for college kids than a little box containing a prepaid phone card or some self-addressed, stamped envelopes and stationery for letters home to the student's family. Keeping in touch helps new students hop the hurdle of homesickness. PowerBars are good too!

PLACING A LOVED ONE IN A NURSING HOME

Prepare a calendar for the child, including stickers, stamps, and cutout hearts. In a note to the child's parents, explain that this calendar can help the child track his or her "sharing of sunshine" with the loved one in the nursing home. Make a plan for happy things the child can do to show the grandparent or other relative that he or she is still thought about, loved, and considered a vital part of the family. Encourage the child to send his loved one pictures of happy times together, special art projects, yummy cookies, and even some stamped self-addressed envelopes for the loved one to send back to the child. If the nursing home allows, take the child for a visit, along with a gentle pet.

NEW BABY

When you visit a new baby, remember to first greet the older child or children. Ask the older child to introduce you to "his" or "her" new baby. When bringing your gift for the newborn, be sure to include a little something for the older child. Books on becoming a new big brother or big sister are a helpful way to ease the stress of a new little person in the home. The older sibling needs to feel just as important as he or she did before the birth of the new family member. Bring a bunch of colorful balloons or a birthday cake for the sibling to celebrate his or her day of becoming a big brother or big sister.

> *Every child born into the world is a new thought of God,*
> *an ever-fresh and radiant possibility.*
>
> —KATE DOUGLAS WIGGIN

MOVING

Send cards to each of the family's children. Ship a little package just after they arrive in their new home as a reminder that someone far away is thinking of them.

ILLNESS IN THE FAMILY

A bundle of books and a sack of snacks make a great pair. Gather up a selection of children's books and place them in a big plastic tote with a lid. The child can even turn the tote upside down and use it for a desk! This works particularly well if little ones have to wait in a hospital room for long periods of time.

Love cures people—both the ones who give it and the ones who receive it.

—KARL MENNINGER

DEATH IN THE FAMILY

Assemble a "you are special" box for the family's children. Include fruits, candies, chips, and other favorite treats, plus an "I love you" note to each child. Place a note in the child's pocket, and tuck in a dollar bill to buy a candy bar, soda, or hot chocolate.

NEW PET

Help the children start a "buddy book" of the family pet. Wrap a small scrapbook in paw print paper and tuck a roll of film in the bow. Include a stamp of a paw print and an inkpad so that each page can be decorated with paw prints as the pet owner fills the "buddy book" with great pictures.

HOLIDAYS AND SPECIAL DAYS

It's a gingerbread man Christmas parade! Prepare or purchase several dozen undecorated gingerbread men, then wrap them in an airtight plastic bag and freeze. (This reduces the stress level for the parents when decorating day arrives.) When you begin your holiday decorating, set aside one day for inviting several children to help you decorate gingerbread men for the Christmas parade.

Cover your table with wax paper or newspaper and gather a bunch of festive decorating items. Decorate the cookies, then set them aside to dry. Spray a preserving spray on the gingerbread men and glue hooks on their backs to use as decorations on the tree. (Be sure to set aside extra cookies for eating! Once sprayed and preserved, the gingerbread men are no longer edible.) If the occasion is not Christmas, have a gingerbread person painting party. Use this as an opportunity to discuss how people are the same on the inside but are all different colors, shapes, and sizes on the outside.

DIVORCE

At this traumatic time in a child's life, it is vital that he or she feels the love and care of others. Many emotions run rampant while this child's little world is totally rearranged. Try putting together a "heartstrings" box. Purchase a heart-shaped box and fill it with heart-shaped items like stickers, stamps, candy, paperweights, soap, and storybooks about love and friendship. Place a note in the box that reads, "Your mommy and daddy really love you, and so do I." You might want to include a book for children that talks about divorce. (I recommend *Divorce Happens to the Nicest Kids* by Michael Prokop, published by Alegra House.)

GOING ON A TRIP

Activity books rolled, tied, and placed in a book bag will help time pass quickly as young travelers wait in a car, airport, or train station. Travel treats and bottled water are also a welcome sight for both parents and children.

CELEBRATING CHILDREN

Declare an outdoors day. Invite some friends, run by a deli, and plan to play. Provide special outdoor games to maximize playtime. You might try having a dads-and-kids game time so the moms can have the opportunity to catch up on conversation, and then reverse the game so the dads can have their social time too.

Life is made up not of great sacrifices or duties, but of little things, in which smiles and kindnesses and small obligations, given habitually, are what win and preserve the heart and secure comfort.

—Sir H. Davy

SIMPLE SOLUTIONS

1. Always look for ways to include your child in your gift giving and sharing.
2. Brainstorm with your child about ways to make a sad friend smile.
3. Make an action plan for sharing. Prepare an easy and age-appropriate plan so that the child may take an active role.
4. When delivering a gift, take the children with you and make them an important part of the delivery.

5. Be a model for your children by sharing your resources with a family less fortunate, donating clothes or supplies to natural-disaster victims, collecting toys for a toy drive, or baking a batch of cookies for a sick neighbor.

CHAPTER THIRTEEN

Gift Giving with Gusto

Love is that condition in which the happiness of another person
is essential to your own joy.

—ROBERT A. HEINLEIN

Gift giving. Just the thought of it can make us nervous. Will the recipient like the gift? Do I have enough in my budget to buy all the gifts I want to give? Must I really go to the mall during the crazy holiday season? Honestly, for years I thought the hoopla surrounding certain days of the year was so stores could make money, and I felt certain a few holidays were created in the marketing office of Hallmark.

Finding that perfect gift is an art form. It's not about what is spent; it is about what is communicated in the process: love.

In Gary Chapman's book *The Five Love Languages*, he shares this: "Gifts come in all sizes, colors, and shapes. Some are expensive, and others are free. To the individual whose primary love language is receiving gifts, the cost of the gift will matter little, unless it is greatly out of line with what you can afford. If a millionaire gives only $1 gifts regularly, the spouse may question whether it is an expression of love. But when family finances are limited, a $1 gift may speak a million dollars worth of love."[1] The key here is listening. Listen to people's interests, hear their hearts, and give as you can.

Gift giving is an important component of hospitality. We show that we care about people when we give them tokens of love and kindness.

HOW TO RECEIVE GIFTS GRACIOUSLY

1. Look the gift giver in the eyes when thanking him or her for the gift.
2. Be genuinely grateful even if you think the gift is atrocious.
3. Share an idea with the giver of how or where you might use the gift item.

RECYCLING A PRESENT

It is not unusual to receive a gift that is either identical to something you already own or not compatible with your needs. When this happens, there is no reason not to pass the present on to a person who, in all probability, would appreciate the article. The item can be placed in an unmarked box or wrapped in tissue paper and placed in a decorative bag. Using the present's original box or the box of another store can be a problem if the recipient chooses to return it and asks the giver for the sales slip, as it could cause embarrassment both to the giver and to the recipient of the present.

Those handmade presents that children often bring home from school: They have so much value! . . . The way we parents respond to the giving of such gifts is very important. To the child the gift is really self, and they want so much for their selves to be acceptable, to be loved.

—FRED ROGERS, *Mister Rogers Talks with Parents*

GIFT GIVING FOR ALL OCCASIONS

With a little planning, gift giving can become a simple expression of your hospitality, no matter what the occasion. For example, at the end of each season, stock up on gift bags, ribbons, and gift cards. This is a time saver when you need a quick yet classy presentation. And never underestimate the simplest form of kindness: one stem of a colorful flower in a petite clear vase, a terrific-smelling home fragrance, or a delectable hand cream.

Here are a few other great gift ideas to get you started:

TOP TEN TEACHER GIFTS

1. A popcorn bowl full of microwave popcorn bags, bottles of Coke, and a gift card for the video store
2. Anything handmade by the entire class
3. Bubble bath and a classical CD
4. A personalized journal
5. Unique glass bottles for bubble bath or for dishwashing soap
6. A glass carafe filled with colorful silk scarves or ties. Add a long straw and a white handkerchief so it resembles a sundae.
7. Eight grapevine wreaths large enough to set dinner plates on. These make interesting place settings.
8. A stocked picnic basket filled with plastic storage containers and nonperishable foods
9. A basket filled with magazines of interest
10. A hatbox full of fruit and a fruit smoothie cookbook

Love worth sharing can be taken to greater heights by your own personality and creations.

—SARAH CABANISS

TOP TEN HOSTESS GIFTS

1. A set of seasonally colored monogrammed tea towels
2. A colorful tin filled with scented votive candles
3. A wrought-iron picture frame—after the dinner or event, send a thank-you note and include a snapshot for the frame
4. Flower bulb subscriptions
5. A galvanized bucket full of daisies
6. A basket filled with assorted jellies
7. A scone mix and a jar of apple butter
8. Unique place card holders

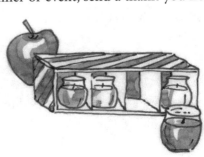

9. A bottle of flavored herb vinegar with a favorite salad dressing recipe tied to the top of the bottle

10. A lip liner and lipstick in the season's most popular color

TOP TWELVE SEASONAL SENSATIONS

January

An exercise book to help a friend stay true to her new year's resolutions. (Tip: only give this gift to someone who has told you about her goal of exercising in the upcoming year. Otherwise, she might hit you with the book you purchased!)

February

Line a large heart-shaped box with plastic wrap and butcher paper. Plant several red tulips in the box. When the tulips wilt, the decorative box will be a pretty keepsake.

March

A colorful kite heralds the coming of spring. This will appeal to the kid in anyone! Be sure the kite has some green on it so the owner won't be pinched!

April

A beautiful umbrella will protect from those April showers. One of the best places to get one is at a museum gift shop. Often they will have prints of famous paintings on the water-repellent material. A relaxation tape of rain and waves would add to your theme.

May

Fruited herbal teas are more popular than ever. This is a perfect time to give some, prior to summer's big tall glasses of iced tea. Try peach, apricot, blackberry, and raspberry flavors.

June

Interesting barbecue sauces add to great summer flavors on the grill. Find unique combinations of flavors for marinades and grilled items. The Salt Lick in Austin,

Texas; Clark's BBQ in Tioga, Texas; and Neiman Marcus with its Red River products sell great barbecue sauces.

July

Red, white, and blue paper products make a fun Independence Day–themed gift. You can find gorgeous paper supplies these days, and everybody needs festive throwaways during the summer.

August

Beach towels make a fun gift when given in large, colorful sand pails you can find at the dollar store.

September

Young kids will enjoy a back-to-school survival kit. Fill a brightly colored pencil box with number-two pencils, erasers, boxes of raisins, and a small packet of tissues.

October

Gourds are decorative heralds of fall. Go to the farmers' market and fill a bushel basket with an assortment of shapes, colors, and sizes of gourds.

November

Thanksgiving means pumpkin pie! Buy your pie instead of making it, but personalize it with a fun topping: Buy some petite cookie cutters in the shapes of leaves, apples, and pumpkins. Buy a prepared piecrust, cut out the shapes on the dough, and bake according to package directions. Top your pie with the piecrust shapes.

December

Busy moms will enjoy receiving this gift! Purchase an inexpensive stockpot at the dollar store. Fill the pot with all the ingredients needed for a beef or chicken stew. Add the recipe to the top. Deliver as your friend arrives home from a big day of shopping.

HUSBANDS MATTER

In this section you will find ideas for fanning the flame of your marriage commitment. My girlfriend Debbie once eloquently said, "Love is like a hothouse flower; it must be cared for and nurtured to stay alive." Hospitality at home matters; extending that kindness to those you see every day builds connection that will last a lifetime.

TOP TEN HUSBAND "HAPPYS"

1. Include a game schedule from his favorite team with his lunch. Even better, include tickets to a home game!
2. Make a batch of homemade play dough and then form a heart shape. Put the imprint of your child's hand in the center and bake to harden. Place a special "I love you" message with the gift.
3. Schedule a golf date and send him a note with details of the time and place.
4. Give him a relaxing music CD along with a special "thinking of you" message to smooth the rough edges of a hectic day at the office.
5. Surprise him with a petite box of designer chocolates with gooey centers.
6. Purchase a big heart sticker and write on the sticker, "You're our hero!"
7. Find a funny cartoon clipping and place it in the seat of his car to lift his harried spirit.
8. Place a couple of movie or concert tickets in a scented envelope and send it to his office.
9. Place a note in his lunchbox inviting him to join the family for a picnic in a beautiful park after work.
10. Ask the kids to create a picture for Daddy's office. Roll up the picture and tie it with a pretty plaid ribbon.

TOP TEN SUPER DATES

1. Have Chinese takeout delivered to your favorite park. Arrive earlier than your food order with a blanket, portable music player, and candles.
2. Plan a one-night excursion to a quaint bed-and-breakfast. Make this a time of total relaxation and conversation so you can catch up on each other's thoughts and feelings.

3. Do a fast-food drive-through progressive dinner. Begin at one of your favorites for an appetizer and end at another for dessert. When you're full—go exercise!

4. Make reservations for an afternoon together at a day spa.

5. Plan an outing to the ocean, lake, pond, or river. Depending on your water source, enjoy a fun activity. You might end up in a canoe, in a fishing boat, or on a dinner cruise.

6. Check out your community theater offerings. If you're near a major city, see if it has a ticket outlet for a great play or musical at a reasonable rate.

7. Experiment with new cuisines. Try a Thai, Vietnamese, or Lebanese restaurant. If you're the adventurous type, rush to the newest sushi bar.

8. Plan an evening at home without the kids. Arrange for the children to stay elsewhere. Rent a romantic video for you and an action-packed video for him. Pop some kettle corn and snuggle on the couch.

9. For a special treat, try a hot-air balloon ride. They usually take off at sunrise, so the romance is built in. If the balloon company does not provide refreshments, take a basket of fruit and cheese with you.

10. Re-create your first date as closely as possible. Go to the same restaurant, rent the same movie, or go to the same theater. If this is impossible, pretend this is your first date. Have your husband leave and come pick you up. Talk to each other as though you've just met. Decide if you are going to kiss him or not!

GIFTS FOR LIFE'S MOMENTS

Occasions, whether happy or sad, are the mortar with which we build the bricks of life. Here are a few ideas for gift giving at some of life's more memorable occasions.

A NEW NEIGHBOR

A thoughtful and sure-to-be appreciated way to offer a helping hand while a new neighbor unloads boxes is to bring a large bag of chipped ice, plastic cups, and bottled water. The overwhelming task of locating their drinking glasses amid the chaos will be solved with this quick pick-me-up!

Now that the practical is solved, the aesthetics can be addressed by cheering up their new house with a beautiful vase full of fragrant fresh flowers or a basket filled with scented candles and potpourri.

JUST BECAUSE YOU'RE MY FRIEND

A stressed-out mom or caregiver needs assistance from time to time. She needs to feel loved, pampered, and appreciated, and you can be the one to make that happen. Give her a coupon for an afternoon (without children) in a favorite bookstore, preferably one that serves coffee and pastries. When she arrives home, have a simple and satisfying dinner ready to pop in the oven so her relaxation can last a little longer. The gift of time is so precious.

CHILDREN GOING TO SCHOOL

When a child is going off to kindergarten, a colorful photo memory album to record the highlights of each school year is a great gift. Place the memory book in a basket filled with freshly baked cookies, hot cocoa mix, and cute mugs.

PLACING A LOVED ONE IN A NURSING HOME

Prepare a sampling of homemade frozen dinners, wrap with butcher paper, and affix labels on the outside of the containers for easy recognition. Include an inspirational book or favorite novel for the person who has placed the loved one in the nursing home to read as he or she reheats and eats the dinners. An emotionally and physically tired person will greatly enjoy this little act of love.

WEDDINGS

Purchase three matching frames. In two of the frames, place pictures of the bride's and groom's parents on their wedding day. Present your gift to the newlyweds, along with a promise to frame their favorite wedding photo to match.

NEW BABY

Purchase a tree from a local nursery and have it planted in the yard of the newborn's home. (Be sure to check with the parents first!) Create a certificate dedicating the tree to the child. Have your picture taken with the child in front of the tree.

MOVING

Send a humorous card to your friends' new address so it is waiting for them when they arrive. Tuck a phone card with several free minutes or hours so they can call and keep you updated on the settling-in progress. Let them know that you will be thinking and praying for them as they adjust to their new home and neighborhood.

ILLNESS IN THE FAMILY

Purchase a clear goldfish bowl from a dollar store. Write on several pieces of paper anything you would do to help the family member who is the main caregiver, like running errands for a day, picking up the children after school, organizing a group of neighbors to bring over dinner several times a week, or setting up a sitter service to help care for the sick person. A simple gesture like keeping the cookie jar full or taking the caregiver out for coffee can help lift spirits. Tie a brightly colored ribbon around the top of the fish bowl and tie a note to it explaining how to redeem each "gift certificate."

DEATH IN THE FAMILY

Purchase some beautiful writing paper in a soft color and write a note to the family telling them how much their loved one meant to you. Include a personal recollection, and don't worry if it happens to be humorous. Family members will enjoy remembering pleasant times.

NEW PET

Purchase a pet picture frame with photos or words describing the pet around the perimeter (available at most pet supply stores). If you are feeling artistic, try taking a regular frame and painting or stenciling paw prints all around the perimeter of it. Place a gift certificate for obedience school or products at the local pet store in the picture part of the frame. Once the gift certificate is removed, pet lovers can put a prized picture of the new family member in the frame. A Christmas ornament with a space for a pet's picture adds a special touch for a happy holiday.

NEW JOB

During your friend's first few days on a new job, make a huge card for the new employee out of butcher paper. Roll out enough paper to cover a door. Write in huge letters, "We are praying for you!" or, "You can do it!" Fill the perimeter of the paper with inspirational quotes and encouraging words. Tape the card to the outside or inside of the door to home or office, whichever is most appropriate. This will be a constant reminder that you are offering needed support.

Another idea is to purchase current magazines that are relevant to your friend's new job. Tie the magazines in a big bundle with a colorful ribbon and deliver the stack to his or her home or office.

HOLIDAYS AND SPECIAL DAYS

Purchase a decorative book that contains blank pages. Fill the book with traditional recipes from generations of your family. On one page, include the recipe, naming it for the relative who makes it or used to prepare it, such as Grandmother Cabaniss's Coconut Pound Cake. On the page opposite the recipe, give a brief biography of that person and your favorite memory or story involving him or her. Prepare a book like this for each member of your family so that they can each have a culinary heirloom.

DIVORCE

Select a box of your friend's favorite tea. Write or type uplifting verses and quotes on decorative paper. Cut the paper into small enough sizes to be stapled to the end of the string on a tea bag. Put each tea bag back into the box and tie a beautiful silk ribbon around it.

GOING ON A SPECIAL TRIP

Fodor's travel books offer a great look at a new city or country. They highlight the best restaurants, activities, and must-sees for the traveler. Enclose a gift certificate for an interesting-sounding restaurant inside your friend's "favorite things" area in the book. Wrap the book with a map of that city or country. If the vacationers already have travel books, give them a lead-lined container for vacation film so it will be protected from airport x-ray machines.

FIFTEEN WAYS TO WRAP GIFTS WITHOUT WRAPPING PAPER

1. Hatboxes: Fill a hatbox with tissue paper, shredded colored paper, or colored cellophane. Place your gift in the center and fill in the empty spaces with your desired stuffing.

2. Wooden Cheese Boxes: Wooden boxes are perfect for stenciling, painting, or monogramming or for gluing on buttons and bows. Try stuffing the inside with a yard of velvet, flannel, or netting, whichever best matches the theme chosen for the outside of your box.

3. Mailing Tubes: You can find mailing tubes in all different colors. Select your favorite and decorate with stamps, stickers, and small ribbons. Fill the inside of the tube with confetti, dried beans, small pine cones, shredded paper, or fabric. Place your gift inside and seal with the lid. (You might want to issue a word of warning before the confetti flies everywhere!)

4. Splatter-Painted Wooden Crates: You can find wooden crates at a farmer's market or at your local grocery store. First, dust off the crates with a towel. Purchase some craft paints with a squirt top, place the crate on some newspaper, and splatter with paint. (Kids love this!) Let dry thoroughly, then line with fabric or raffia.

5. Aluminum Foil: Pull out several long sheets of foil, place your gift in the center, pull the foil around the gift, and twist like a chocolate kiss. Tuck a note in the top of the chocolate kiss. This is a great gift-wrap for a chocolate lover.

6. Glass Carafes: Fill a glass carafe halfway with little pebbles, small shells, pennies, or corn kernels. Place a small gift in the middle and fill the rest with pebbles, shells, fresh cranberries, or whatever filler you choose until the gift is covered. Place a small handkerchief on the top of the carafe and secure it with a rubber band and a colorful ribbon. This will be like finding a prize in a Cracker Jack box.

7. Galvanized Buckets: Fill the inside of the bucket with raffia, shredded paper or crumpled tissue paper, or various colors of yarn. Tie a large bow around the perimeter of the bucket. Load up with favorite food items, a CD, and bubble bath.

8. Chinese Takeout Containers: Line the inside of a Chinese takeout container with cellophane or raffia. Place your gift inside, close the container, and tie the top with a large ribbon.

9. Burlap Bags: Line the inside of a burlap bag with fabric. Tie the bag with raffia or a ribbon.

10. Canning Jars: Remove several labels from cans in your pantry. Place them facing outward around the perimeter of the glass canning jar so the gift will remain a mystery until opened.

11. Hollowed-Out Pumpkin: Line a hollowed-out pumpkin with green florist paper or plastic wrap. Fill individual plastic bags with the dry ingredients for pumpkin-cranberry bread. Top the pumpkin with its lid and tie the recipe to the stem.

12. Clear Acrylic Boxes: Line the box with florist paper, tissue, or newspaper. Top with a lid and place a large ribbon under the bottom of the box, tying a bow at the top. (Fabric ribbon that has wire on both edges makes the best bow.)

13. Colored Netting: Fabric stores have great wrapping paper alternatives! Buy about a yard of netting, depending on the size of the gift. Place the gift inside and pull the netting over the gift. Secure with a rubber band and tie with a long piece of rickrack.

14. Mixing Bowl and Food Section: Fill the mixing bowl with ingredients of a favorite recipe. Cover the top of the bowl with the food section from your newspaper and secure with kitchen twine or a large dishcloth.

15. Little Themed Boxes: Many stores sell boxes in the shape of gingerbread men, stars, hearts, and bunnies. Fill the inside of a themed box with cookies to match the theme. Little gingerbread men placed in baking papers and then in a matching box will make a perfect "thinking of you" gift, no matter what the occasion.

Advice is cheap. . . . It's the things that come gift-wrapped that count.
—HORACE VANDERGELDER IN *Hello, Dolly!*

SAYING THANKS

1. Make your thank-you note personal. If your penmanship is presentable, opt for a handwritten note.
2. Dispatch your thanks within one to three days of receiving a gift.
3. If you're really late sending off your note, don't give any excuses. Moaning about how busy you are undermines the gesture. Don't mention your lateness at all.
4. Be creative about how you say thanks. Think outside the flower box. Or the mailbox. Or the chocolate box.
5. Do a little investigating. Call a few mutual friends to find out if the generous person has a hobby or an interest. Proceed accordingly.
6. If you are not sure whether you were generous enough with your initial show of gratitude, send a follow-up card at holiday time.[2]

SIMPLE SOLUTIONS

If you have a "go-to" list of simple gift ideas, you will never be stuck when needing a quick pick-me-up for another person. Here's a good start:

1. An assortment of fresh herbs tied with natural-colored raffia
2. A box of brightly colored Christmas balls, which look terrific in a large crystal bowl
3. Store-bought sugar-cookie dough and some assorted mix-ins, such as mini M&Ms, dried cranberries, pistachios, or crystallized ginger
4. A coloring book of the hottest new character and a package of fat crayons
5. Unusual refrigerator magnets
6. An assortment of nuts in a brightly colored glass decanter
7. A paperweight with personality
8. A dozen paper-white bulbs nestled in pebbles in an interesting clay pot

CHAPTER FOURTEEN

Bedside Manners

The smallest acts of kindness are worth more than the grandest intention.
—UNKNOWN

When a friend tells you she is engaged, you know exactly how to respond. When another gets a big promotion, you want all the details ("Did you get the corner office?"). But when a friend or family member faces a serious health problem, suddenly we can be at a loss for how to help or what to do.

In her book *The Etiquette of Illness*, Susan P. Halpern describes this dilemma: "I stand with my hand on the receiver. I want to call my friend who has just been diagnosed with lupus, but my mind has reverted to that of a seven year old, and an inner tape plays. What am I going to say? How am I going to say it? . . . Just the simple phrase, 'I don't know what to say' can be the catalyst and everything will flow from there."[1]

The difficult times of life are simple hospitality's most tender moments. Often we feel awkward and uneasy around someone who is ill. We don't want to say the wrong thing or act unaffected by their trial, but we don't want to mess up either. Our biggest charge in difficult situations boils down to compassion and common sense. We can't just clam up and do nothing. In this chapter, we are going to take some thoughts and advice from experts on illness and recovery, and we will explore helpful words and actions for situations when a loved one's well-being—physical and emotional—is the issue. Remember, good bedside manners aren't just for doctors.

In Henri Nouwen's book *Our Greatest Gift: Meditations on Dying and Caring,* he shares this wisdom:

> Our society suggests that caring and living are quite separate and that caring belongs primarily to professionals who have received special training. Although training is important, and although certain people need preparation to practice their profession with competence, caring is the privilege of every person and is at the heart of being human. When we look at the original meaning of the word *profession* and realize that the term refers, first of all, to professing one's own deepest conviction, then the essential spiritual unity between living and caring becomes clear. . . . Caring is helping others to claim for themselves the spiritual truth that they are—as we are—children of God, brothers and sisters of each other, and parents of generations to come.[2]

SIGNED, SEALED, AND DELIVERED

Caring is a building block of hospitality, and it comes in a variety of simple, encouraging forms. Cards, notes, and letters can be powerful ways to send encouragement. A card to a sick person or shut-in can be the difference between an okay day and a banner day. It feels so good to know that someone took a minute to say, "You matter, and you are loved." I can remember one difficult day when I received a card with a hilarious middle-aged lady on the front and a funny message inside from one of my friends. I laughed and laughed—just what the doctor ordered. Humor in the mail is a simple gesture with a powerful punch.

A card ministry is a timely tool. Just drop a note saying, "I prayed for you today." Simple. Meaningful. Poignant. Many churches offer this ministry to their members. If your church does not have this, why not start one? Gather a list of those who are hurting, missionaries overseas, men and women in the service. Call it Day Lifters, a ministry with a mission. Just think how many we could touch with a stack of cards and some stamps!

PHONE FELLOWSHIP

Being heard is paramount when we need to feel loved. Pick up the phone. Call. You don't need to talk for hours—just a few minutes is enough to say, "I'm thinking of you today. Have a blessed day."

Phone prayer chains are another powerful way to offer support to a hurting person. You have a point person start the request. They call you, then you call the next person on the list, and so on until all the prayer partners have been called. Prayer chains send powerful petitions to heaven while offering peace to all participants.

SIMPLE HOSPITALITY FOR THE HURTING

Often we can best comfort others in silence. Sometimes no words seem right, and there is a heartfelt way to say nothing at all. Alexandra explained, "The day of my sister's funeral, my friend Julia came over. She did not say anything. She just gave me this incredible hug, and I remember it to this day." Silence. Presence. Prayers. Fumbling for futile expressions is often unnecessary.

When people are hurting, hospitality has very little to do with cute ideas and clever food combinations; it has to do with time, sincere concern, and constantly gauging what the family in the "hot seat" might need when they have no idea of their needs. Simply put, hospitality to the hurting boils down to heart listening—being and not doing. This is a life lesson for me, the "doer": when others are hurting, I just need to *be* with them, to observe while being willing to take on whatever task seems urgent at the moment.

Let's look at a few circumstances where simple hospitality to the hurting can be shared in silence, in words, or in deed.

MISCARRIAGE

The death of a dream is how I describe a miscarriage. First you're up and then you're down, and your heart goes around and around—those hormones misfiring all over the place. The sadness for what might have been is quite a hurdle. Even now when people ask me, "You just have one child?" I get an urge to explain my entire medical history, but I refrain and realize God is in control.

In her book *Moments for Couples Who Long for Children*, Ginger Garrett describes the excruciating experience of miscarriage: "As the ultrasound technician passed the sonogram wand over my belly, her face revealed the terrible truth. The baby was gone. At that moment I was initiated into a sorority I never wanted to join: the group of women who have lost children before their time."[3]

So how does one offer hospitality for this hurt? A warm embrace and a listening spirit meet the mark when dealing with this type of pain. Try not to say things like, "You might have been saved from having a child with a terrible difficulty" or, "You can always try again." In the heart of a mom, every child is precious, and the one lost must be mourned. Those words can be comforting coming from a doctor, but as a friend, you're better off just being there and expressing your sorrow for the loss. Just ask, "How are you feeling?" Simple kindness.

DIVORCE

Divorce is like a death, but the other person is still walking around. The severing of an emotional bond that was supposed to be "till death do us part" is excruciating. Divorce takes its toll in the depths of your heart. How do we offer comfort and kindness to someone in this situation?

Assume a nonjudgmental attitude and listen. Be a cheerleader, offer encouragement, and assist your friend in reviewing all his or her options for a different future. Keep an eye on your friend; don't let her bury herself in her own burdens. Share with her often that there is light after this darkness.

LOSS OF A JOB

Losing a job is not only a financial blow, but it is also a blow to the self-esteem. First shock sets in, and then hope for that new position, and then the waiting game. The best hospitality is to first listen to the family as they share their feelings, then ask if they want your help or just a listening ear. If they're open to assistance, start with networking and contact everyone you know who might have a lead for your job-hunting friend.

Offer constant encouragement, such as books on tape, devotions full of hope, e-mails of positive quotes, and if time allows, a weekly coming together for prayer. Don't say, "It's all for the best." Let your friend come to that conclusion on his or her own, however much time it takes.

HOSPITAL STAY

A hospitalized person needs an advocate to interpret what the doctor says. If lots of family members are visiting at staggered times, you can avoid mass confusion and repetitive recaps by appointing a family spokesperson. This cuts down on the doctor's having to repeat information, and it helps to avoid conflicting and confusing information. Any way we can ease the stress, avoid confusion, and help the loved one is an act of caring, a gift of hospitality.

Recently while my mother was in the hospital for an extended stay, I asked several doctors how family and friends might be of significant assistance to the staff and the patient in time of illness. Here are some of their suggestions:

- Keep a journal at the patient's bedside to keep track of the day's events, new medications, and the prognosis. It also helps as a central place for writing down questions you need answered.
- Keep a list of questions handy. You stay on track in your thought process while getting all the information you need.
- If you have concerns over the quality of care given by a hospital staff member, don't be afraid to say something.
- If you have problems with the doctor, first talk with the nurse to see if she might be of help. If the concern continues, a hospital social worker can be of assistance.

TERMINAL ILLNESS

Offering your time is the most precious gift to those who know their time is limited. Use your common sense in determining how to help. You can do mundane chores like get ice for the patient and candy from the vending machine for everybody in the room. Find out the little somethings to make the patient and the caregivers feel loved. Things like Chewy Sweetarts, candy corn, cookies, and a little note let the person know he or she is being thought about.

My sister-in-law Susie was a giver of this type of hospitality for more than fifteen months to a neighbor family. Her best advice is this: "Follow your heart and do what makes sense to you. The goal is to make the person feel special." Often the sick person feels like a burden to others and as though they are taking valuable life moments from the family and friends they love. We can lift the burden, even if only for a few minutes, by being available, actively listening, and finding practical ways to help.

Terminally ill persons have the same physical, emotional, and spiritual needs as everyone else; but in addition, they often are concerned about being abandoned, losing control over their bodies and lives, and being in overpowering pain or distress. What they need most of all is to be cared *about*, not just cared for. Many of their needs can be met by anyone: gently holding their hand, softly singing their favorite hymns, reminiscing about some favorite times together. Follow your heart and ask Jesus, the maker of peace and comfort, to be present.

When you're considering the simple ways you might offer hospitality to a friend or loved one, think about the four main areas of care for those who are coping with dying: physical, psychological, social, and spiritual. The family members and friends of the dying person, as well as professional and volunteer caregivers, have these needs as well.

DELICACY OF DIGNITY

When an illness takes its toll on a patient's ability to think clearly, it is a painful loss for the family and for the patient. My friend Elise's mother was very ill. She had broken her hip and seemed to be recovering nicely—until one day she seemed fine, and the next she was disoriented and unable to clearly communicate. The entire family was in shock. The mom knew she was slipping in and out of cognitive ability and would discuss it when her thoughts were lucid. The doctors could not explain exactly what was happening.

Elise explained, "The hardest part is looking in my mother's eyes and seeing that intelligent, vibrant, and humorous woman I knew, but hearing thoughts, words, and expressions that make no sense. You have to pull from deep within to conquer your emotions while offering empathy and love for the person who is slowly losing her capacity to think."

A most significant gift of hospitality in its simplest form is offering the dying the dignity they deserve. Oftentimes this involves protecting them from visitors when you know the ill person would not want to be seen or heard during a rough day. This can be done with polite expressions, by signs on the door asking for no visitors, and by asking well-wishers to offer a kind gesture to the caregiver. The cycle of life can be rough, but the power of prayer can carry you through.

COMFORT FOR KIDS

- Shoot the news straight with a child, using age-appropriate information.
- Choose the right time of day to discuss the matter, when the child is not tired or distracted.
- Help the child understand that the illness may mean a change in the child's routine.
- Let teachers, friends, and baby-sitters know what you are dealing with so they might help you look for signs of stress in the child.
- Try not to assure the child that everything is going to be okay if it is not.
- When a death occurs, let the child know it is okay to be sad, mad, or scared.
- Assist the child in doing something special for the loved one. Even in tough times, a gentle touch or a sweet laugh from a child can be like sunshine after a bad storm.
- Be sure to answer any questions the child asks. This will help to keep them from feeling uncertain.

SIMPLE SOLUTIONS

1. People often receive an avalanche of attention when they first get sick. Remember to check in with the person later on, as treatment or recovery continues.
2. Books and magazines make great gifts for someone in the hospital. Keep the subject matter light, and look for material that can be read in short spurts.
3. If a family member is going to be in the hospital for a long period of time, become well acquainted with the hospital staff. Extend them the hospitality you would like extended to your loved one.

4. Start an e-mail list of friends and prayer partners. Update everyone at once on the treatments and progress of the ill person. This is extremely helpful to the family and keeps them from answering the same questions over and over again.

5. Drop off food. Prepare something that will keep or that can be frozen. Use disposable containers so no returning is necessary.

6. Assist in the home with laundry, cleaning, or grocery shopping. This is a good time to show up with helping hands.

7. Look for ways to care for the caregiver. Offer to stay with the loved one so the caregiver can go to a movie, take a long walk, or go to the mall.

8. Offer to drive to doctors' appointments.

9. Send a manicurist to the hospital to pamper the patient.

10. Prepare a big bowl of fresh fruit for the patient and visitors.

Epilogue

The word *home* warms our hearts and reminds us of a place that is safe and accepting no matter the circumstance. As I was writing this book, I understood the meaning of *home* in an entirely new way. We decided to put our home "on the market"—a catch phrase meaning that anyone desiring a new place or a Sunday afternoon jaunt might come by to view your personal establishment, your collected stuff, and your ability to create an environment that another would deem purchasable.

To me, selling your home is selling a part of yourself. A home is a part of who you are—even when it is not picture perfect. As I pressed the send button for this manuscript, I was contractually homeless. We had put our house up for sale (or for critique) at the same time as we put a contract on our new home. As the days marched forward, we decided our new place needed more attention than we had resources, so we canceled the contract. In the meantime, our current home was sold and severed from our creative expressions and warm, fuzzy feelings. To heighten matters, this all happened just prior to Christmas. When most people were wrapping gifts, we were signing contracts and moving into a temporary apartment, awaiting our new home.

What does this experience have to do with hospitality? Plenty! This Christmas we had no home, only a newly rented apartment and limited time to deck the halls. Yet I was determined to have a fresh pine tree and all the festivities of Christmas. As the wife and mother still in charge of setting the tone of the living environment, I wanted to create a place that felt like home, smelled like home, looked like home, and tasted like home even though it was not the home we had known just a few days earlier. Simple hospitality in its finest hour was born. How? By assuming the mode of sheer simplicity. We packed everything but the essentials, purposed to view our lifestyle as positive, and proceeded to make the best of the situation.

I learned when one lights a fragrant votive candle, places some store-bought cookie dough in the oven, and sets the table with decorative paper products, the feeling of home appears. A wreath on the door and a small plant at the entryway offer a welcoming feeling to your guests. Classical music wafting through the air adds coziness. Most of all, creating a hospitable attitude whatever your circumstance is key.

Simple hospitality is part of our ministry whether we feel it is our specific spiritual bent or not. As we have seen in these chapters, hospitality is more than menus, unique décor, and showmanship. Hospitality means making room for one more, always an extra place at the table or an extra pillow and blanket, always an offer of encouragement whatever the circumstance. It means scheduling time for a planned get-together and setting aside other plans for impromptu gatherings. This is not always easy to do, but practicing hospitality is not God's suggestion; it is God's command. As I have mentioned, the spirit of hospitality will come full circle when we least expect it.

Can a home that truly lives in the heart be temporarily transported? You bet! But it takes work, hope, and personal determination. We had company right away in our apartment—our daughter's friends. Why? Because our nine-year-old needed to see that hospitality did not require a home, a fancy setting, or a permanent address; it required a heart reaching out to another, whether a friend or a new acquaintance. For our first dinner in the apartment, we invited my parents and served food on our Christmas china. We purposed to use that china all during Christmas just because it is pretty. A small place with fresh smells, good food, and warm conversation is the essence of real hospitality. We will continue to invite others and be thankful for those who helped ease the pain of moving.

Fellowship with one another can happen no matter the location, color of the walls, or financial status. Simple hospitality does not require exceptional surroundings or outstanding ability; it only requires kindness and a willing heart.

NOTES

Introduction: Pure Hospitality
1. *Webster's Dictionary,* s.v. "Hospitality."

Chapter 1: Clean Plate Club
1. Charles Hummel, *Freedom from Tyranny of the Urgent* (Wheaton, Ill.: InterVarsity, 1997).

Chapter 2: The Simple Truth
1. Shirley Kane Lewis, *On the Journey Towards Hospitality.*

Chapter 3: Homeland Hospitality
1. Karen Mains, *Open Heart, Open Home* (Downers Grove, Ill.: InterVarsity, 2002).

Chapter 4: Beyond Harried Holidays
1. Ann Hibbard, *Family Celebrations at Easter* (Grand Rapids, Mich.: Baker, 1994).

Chapter 5: Faking Homemaking
1. Marla Cilley, *Sink Reflections* (New York: Bantam, 2002).
2. Ibid.

Chapter 7: The Kitchen Magician
1. Dixie Cook, interview with author. Used by permission.

Chapter 9: Designing an Inviting Entrance
1. Chris Madden, *Chris Madden's Guide to Personalizing Your Home* (New York: Clarkson Potter, 1997).

Chapter 10: Maximizing Ministry Moments

1. *Merriam-Webster's Collegiate Dictionary,* tenth edition s.v. "Share."

2. *Merriam-Webster's,* s.v. "Minister."

3. Rick Warren, *The Purpose Driven Life* (Grand Rapids, Mich.: Zondervan, 2002), 281.

4. Mindy Short, e-mail to author. Used by permission.

Chapter 12: Kid Connection

1. For more information about Samaritan's Purse and Operation Christmas Child, call 1-800-353-5949 or go to www.SamaritansPurse.org.

Chapter 13: Gift Giving with Gusto

1. Gary Chapman, *The Five Love Languages* (Chicago: Moody, 1996).

2. Letitia Baldrige, *New Manners for New Times: A Complete Guide to Etiquette* (New York: Scribner, 2003).

Chapter 14: Bedside Manners

1. Susan P. Halpern, *The Etiquette of Illness: What to Say When You Can't Find the Words* (New York: Bloomsbury, 2004).

2. Henri Nouwen, *Our Greatest Gift: Meditations on Dying and Caring* (San Francisco: HarperSanFrancisco, 1995).

3. Ginger Garrett, *Moments for Couples Who Long for Children* (Colorado Springs: NavPress, 2004).